Special Praise for *21st Century Parenting*

"Although there are numerous parenting primers on the market, this book offers a unique perspective on what parents need to know at this particular moment in time. It provides parents with a roadmap to raise successful children who are dealing with unprecedented challenges and temptations. Each chapter contains information that is clear, practical, and succinct. For parents raising children in the twenty-first century, this book is indispensable."

Bernard Schwartz, PhD
Founder and Director of Student Psychological
Services at Santiago Canyon College
Author of *How to Fail as a Therapist*

"It has been our honor and privilege at Mater Dei High School to have had the opportunity and blessing to work with Dr. Rick Capaldi and Outreach Concern for more than twenty-five years.

Dr. Capaldi's book is an 'easy read' with clear, reasonable, and powerful recommendations to help kids cope with the pressures of today's instant gratification world of social media, texting, and online everything. From the Power of Paying Attention to Redirecting Your Child's/Student's Behavior to Parental Leadership, Dr. Rick Capaldi provides a treasure trove of practical real-world approaches.

I want to personally thank and congratulate Dr. Capaldi for writing such an outstanding book that will serve and help so many adults support and guide thousands and thousands of children in becoming more emotionally resilient in a world that is unstable, fast paced, and pressurized for the youth of today. This is an exceptional book for parents, teachers, and mental health professionals at a time when we *all* need the thoughtful and practical parenting guidelines outlined in *21st Century Parenting*."

Patrick Murphy
President of Mater Dei High School

"*21st Century Parenting* is a dynamic resource for parents, which offers a blend of proactive ideas and supportive recommendations for a wide variety of current needs for our children. Rick offers accessible strategies and approaches to parenting that can serve as guideposts, or 'parenting GPS' tools as he describes it, for navigating many issues including the culture of school, using technology, bullying, and building independence in our children that allow them to thrive and be successful as teens and young adults. As an educator, I appreciate the easy to navigate suggestions and, as a parent of two adult sons, I wish I had access to this resource many years before!"

Jennifer Shepard
Assistant Superintendent
Huntington Beach School District

"In an age when parenting has become an increasingly difficult task, *21st Century Parenting* offers a refreshing, practical approach to empower parents with the tools they need to guide their children in a complex world. Dr. Rick Capaldi has developed an evidenced-based model to effectively foster resilience in children as they navigate their environment at home and in school. Key to this model is a parent's awareness of Core Development Competencies that can help their children with the daily interactions with others and work to resolve conflict. Through a better understanding, regular monitoring, and strategic intervention, parents will be in a better position to raise healthy, well-adjusted, and resilient children. Dr. Capaldi's results-based strategies along with practical examples provide parents with a model for success.

Richard McAlindin
Director of Executive Services
Placentia-Yorba Linda Unified School District

"Compliment the child's real accomplishments and don't celebrate what you don't see because no one else will is a truth that Dr. Capaldi is willing to speak, but few parents are ready to hear. This book intelligently presents a blueprint for parents and teachers to be assets in helping children build self-confidence through emotional resilience. In *21st Century Parenting*

resilient, and ultimately, a confident self-reliant young adult. Unlike most parenting books that are based solely on child developmental theory, *21st Century Parenting* shares what works from a wealth of child and family counseling experience and case study observation.

With several decades of student and family counseling experience, Dr. Capaldi and his team have seen it all, heard it all, and gained much insight about what it takes to support today's youngsters in their journey to adulthood. He extracts and distills his team's knowledge and experience to provide parents a straightforward framework, practical tools, and guidance to foster understanding and effective support for their child's development to become a resilient and successful student, adolescent, and adult.

For nearly two decades I've had the opportunity to witness the work of Dr. Capaldi and his staff to successfully aid students and families. *21st Century Parenting* captures not only the critical role parents play in guiding their child's success, but also key parenting strategies that cement parent-child trust and, over time, positively impact the child and the family's future."

Greg Magnuson
Retired Superintendent of Buena Park, California School District

"*21st Century Parenting* is timely and greatly needed. Dr. Capaldi identifies and addresses the current concerns that affect today's families. He outlines essential concepts that are necessary to promote resiliency in children and utilizes anecdotal examples to promote greater understanding. His convincing arguments for parental participation and explicit parental leadership are vital protective factors to manage the ever-increasing anxieties in children who are both distracted and influenced by social media and the addictive use of technology. One of the helpful tools is the parenting GPS that offers four approaches for consideration. Finally, this book offers parents, grandparents, and other caretakers a well-defined roadmap to raise confident, competent, and resilient children in an ever-changing world."

Debra Hill, EdD
Director, Safe Schools, Healthy Students
Westminster United School District

we are educated in the contemporary 3Rs—Learning to *Read* the child's needs and intentions, help the child learn to *Regulate* his or her behaviors, and guiding the child in *Redirecting* his or her energy. The new information presented here—a research consolidation of years of treatment and thousands of in vivo treatment hours—sets a new standard for promoting an emotionally healthy child. This is an essential read for all parents and school personnel."

Samuel Dambrocia, PhD
Psychologist, APC

"Dr. Capaldi addresses challenging issues in a thought-provoking style that is both easy to read and engaging from the first page. We all want to protect our child from the dangers of the world; however, most of us are simply overwhelmed by the hectic pace of daily life and don't have a plan of action on how to navigate through the many issues our child faces on a day-to-day basis.

Dr. Capaldi's plan provides a 'Parenting GPS' to help you guide your child through his daily life, with a focus on both the daily struggles and the long-term goals. We've all heard of the three Rs: reading, 'riting, and 'rithmatic. Dr. Capaldi proposes a new set of Rs: reading your child's environment, regulating your child's emotional temperature, and redirecting your child's behavior.

Dr. Capaldi's years of success as a family therapist, his scientific approach to parenting, and his proven track record showing real behavioral improvements in thousands of children who have been guided by him combine to make this book the best parenting book I have seen. As a brain scientist and a mother, I urge you to begin the life-changing process of learning the new parenting skills presented in *21st Century Parenting*."

Nicole M. Gage, PhD
Former Director of Cognitive Neuroscience
of Language Laboratory, UC Irvine
Author of *Fundamentals of Cognitive Neuroscience: A Beginner's Guide*

"*21st Century Parenting* is a timely and high impact resource for parents to support their most important responsibility—raising their child to become

21st Century Parenting

21ST Century PARENTING

A Guide to Raising Emotionally Resilient
Children in an Unstable World

Rick Capaldi

CENTRAL RECOVERY PRESS
LAS VEGAS

Central Recovery Press (CRP) is committed to publishing exceptional materials addressing addiction treatment, recovery, and behavioral healthcare topics.

For more information, visit www.centralrecoverypress.com.

Publisher: Central Recovery Press
3321 N. Buffalo Drive
Las Vegas, NV 89129

24 23 22 21 20 19   1 2 3 4 5

Library of Congress Cataloging-in-Publication Data
Names: Capaldi, Rick, author.
Title: 21st century parenting: raising emotionally resilient children in an
   unstable world / Rick Capaldi, Ph.D.
Description: Las Vegas, NV: Central Recovery Press, [2019] |
Identifiers: LCCN 2018057894 (print) | LCCN 2019007225 (ebook) | ISBN
   9781949481013 (ebook) | ISBN 9781949481006 (pbk: alk. paper)
Subjects: LCSH: Parenting--Psychological aspects. | Parent and child. |
   Emotions in children. | Internet and children--Safety measures.
Classification: LCC BF723.P25 (ebook) | LCC BF723.P25 C37 2019 (print) | DDC
   649/.1--dc23
LC record available at https://lccn.loc.gov/2018052579

Photo of Rick Capaldi by Don Romero. Used with permission.

Publisher's Note: This book contains general information about parenting, family dynamics, and related matters. The information is not medical advice. This book is not an alternative to medical advice from your doctor or other professional healthcare provider.

All identifying details, including names, have been changed except for those that pertain to the author's colleagues and family members. This book is not intended as a substitute for working with a trained professional.

Our books represent the experiences and opinions of their authors only. Every effort has been made to ensure that events, institutions, and statistics presented in our books as facts are accurate and up-to-date.

Cover design and interior by Deb Tremper, Six Penny Graphics.

To my parents, Fredrick and Emogene

TABLE OF CONTENTS

Preface

Wouldn't it be great if there were a Parent App on your phone to feed you useful data about how your children are doing, alert you when they're veering off the rails (or headed over a cliff!), and help you take quick effective action to get them safely back on track?

In our fast-paced, competitive world, millions of children struggle to maintain their emotional stability and grow up feeling safe, secure, and confident. And often no one notices until it's too late. So, what makes it too late? Often, distracted parents are missing the signals of children in distress.

Children are very good at hiding their pain. However, they often telegraph it in subtle ways as well, which is why parents need to become more effective at reading such signals before their kids go astray. If your kids' emotional backpacks become too heavy and you don't notice, your children can embark on a progressive downward spiral prompting them to make decisions that sabotage their well-being and performance, both in and out of school.

Today, our kids face challenges and dangers that we never dreamed of when we were growing up: online predators; mass school shootings; vicious cyberbullying that can lead to anxiety, depression, and/or suicidal behavior. In addition, they spend more time staring into screens than we ever imagined possible, absorbing an incredible amount of information largely beyond our control. The consequences of these influences and societal pressures can be truly horrifying. It's a stark reminder of the need for parents to pay attention.

If you're like most parents, you probably struggle with determining the best way to guide your children. Where's that "App" that provides insight into what's going on in their heads and what direction you should take to intervene before their actions negatively impact their lives and the lives of others?

Well, here's the news, for good or bad: the only "Parent App" your family can actually depend on or should ever need is *you*. Why? Because parenting is personal. It calls for intimate engagement. Technology may be the answer for many of today's challenges, but it can't take the place of the most important job parents will ever have: being the most important and influential people in the lives of their children.

You can't tweet, Google, Facetime, Instagram, or Snapchat your way to developing a successful family. In short, there's no substitute for moms and dads doing their jobs. That was one of my reasons for writing *21st Century Parenting*.

21st Century Parenting provides you with clear direction to enable you to *read*, *regulate*, and *redirect* your child's behavior—today's core parental principles—that can ensure your child's safety and success.

21st Century Parenting is supported with compelling real-world cases from my lengthy career as a family therapist specializing in counseling families, children, and teens. It provides parents with a "Parenting GPS" to guide their kids successfully through the many turns, roadblocks, and detours from childhood to adulthood. It is intended as a practical guide that avoids many of the common "myths" about what causes childhood emotional problems such as low self-esteem. It keeps parents from becoming roadblocks in their child's journey toward success; helps parents establish parental leadership; and provides tested tools to support their children's educational and emotional potential. It demonstrates how parents can protect their children from being bullied or becoming victims of technology, and provides tools to effectively launch children into becoming adult success stories.

Most importantly, these claims aren't based on theories. The methods incorporated in *21st Century Parenting* have been tested with thousands of children and teens in hundreds of schools through my nonprofit school-based counseling program, Outreach Concern Inc., which has a proven twenty-six-year track record of success in improving the emotional stability, behavior, and academic performance of children.

In September 1993, Outreach Concern, Inc. opened its doors with the mission to provide a cost-effective, comprehensive program of counseling and support services in schools and to positively impact a child's emotional well-being and performance.

We began providing those services in twelve schools with fourteen counselors and limited financial support. In those early years, things were difficult for a small nonprofit agency with a new idea, but our reputation grew as we attained positive outcomes for our clients, and more and more schools adopted our program.

Today, Outreach Concern has been incorporated in over 894 public and private elementary, middle, and high schools. We have served over 500,000 children, parents, and families, provided over two million hours of intervention, and trained over 9,000 mental health professionals. After a quarter-century of service, we have become one of the largest nonprofit, school-based counseling agencies in the country with a story and results that need to be told.

Working with over 3,200 children each week, we see thousands of children and families who've experienced mental health issues, economic setbacks, divorce, emotional, social, and academic instability, or are just in need of help in raising their children. Over time, our work with these clients has led to the development of a new parent/child intervention model focused on improving performance. This established the basis for *21st Century Parenting,* identifying what parents need to know in order to raise healthy, well-adjusted, successful children today and in the future.

Early in Outreach's journey, we became dissatisfied with traditional counseling programs and methods that required lengthy time commitments and great expense, lacked specific goals, and often produced poor outcomes. As a result, we sought to develop an intervention model that focused on *rapid behavioral change* through a more direct, strategic, and controlled approach—one with measurable results—that addressed the present needs of children and adolescents in school and at home with parents as the main force in their child's life.

In this process we came to recognize that contrary to popular belief it isn't a lack of self-esteem, confidence, or motivation that negatively affect a child's performance; rather, it's the *lack of performance* and *accomplishments* a child demonstrates that give rise to feelings of inadequacy, leading to a further unwillingness to challenge himself, and ultimately establishes a child's negative personal identity. And that lack of accomplishment results from parents not being engaged with their children. By not paying sufficient attention to what's going on in their child's world, not equipping him or her with the necessary tools to respond effectively when emotional temperatures rise, and not properly directing their child's efforts to promote accomplishments, parents are responsible for whether their children fail or succeed.

We concluded that successful, emotionally stable children with high self-esteem typically have parents who do the following:

- Pay close attention to what's going on in their child's world— emotionally, academically, socially, and behaviorally;
- Equip their children with the necessary tools to respond effectively to emotional challenges; and
- Direct their children's efforts toward accomplishments, driving them to their highest level of competency.

The Outreach model provided a new blueprint of how school counselors can be effective—not by focusing solely on the child, but by partnering with the most important people in the child's life: the parents.

Our success was further evidenced by the results of a nine-year Student Performance Accountability Study (see study at www.outreachconcern.org) involving 30,662 student referrals from elementary through high school. Each year in the schools we work in, teachers and parents were asked to rate student academic performance and behavior since counseling was initiated focusing on GPA (grade point average) and behavioral improvement. Overall, survey results have indicated an 87 percent performance improvement in academic, behavioral, and psychological domains of those children seen by our counselors.

Those numbers are impressive, supporting the effectiveness of the intervention model we developed. Our next challenge was to assess whether those children seen by our counselors continued to demonstrate the changes our model produced over an extended period of time. Incorporating a five-year longitudinal study following 6,784 students from sixty-five elementary, middle, and high schools, we identified only 19 percent—1,265 of the original student referrals—were re-referred back to our counselors for similar or related issues.

An equally significant aspect of our findings was that in 97 percent of the children who demonstrated improvement, parental participation was a key factor. Once our counselors provided parents with specific guidance and the appropriate tools, their children's performance and behavior improved significantly. *21st Century Parenting* describes in detail how parents can use these same tools developed through the Outreach Concern program to improve performance and stronger parent-child relationships.

Our methods, which have produced thousands of success stories with children and families, led to the development of one of the most comprehensive school-based counseling programs in the country and established a new foundation for parenting in the twenty-first century based on one simple truth: parents still need to matter the most in the lives of their children.

Of course, the success parents achieve incorporating *21st Century Parenting* doesn't come easily. It relies on a parent's commitment to embrace a leadership style that, at times, may make them a bit less popular with their children—the result of making tough, unpopular decisions that are always, however, in the best interest of their family.

As the most significant and influential person in your child's life, you, the parent, get to determine what that interest is. And it is of utmost importance that you recognize that no matter what age, experience, or success your children achieve, your parental responsibility never ends. It only changes, acting as a perpetual counterbalance to the various influences your children are exposed to, influences that may sometimes present challenges and opportunities contrary to their best interest. This is why parents need to pay attention.

21st Century Parenting provides parents a new, dynamic, highly successful approach to such challenges, one that incorporates parents, children, and other significant position-holders in a child's life, with a focus on improving behavior, performance, and parent-child relationships. In this way we can encourage children to thrive in the world as adults, helping them to make it a better place for themselves and future generations.

This begins by paying attention to what children really need—and that does not mean having the latest cell phones, iPads, or video games. It does, however, mean having parents who are empowered by the tools provided in *21st Century Parenting*. Tools that can help parents develop capable, sensitive, and resilient children into successful adults.

The Power of Paying Attention

"When you really pay attention, everything is your teacher."
—EZRA BAYDA

Before considering a new approach to raising your children, you have the right to ask why? Our experience has shown that many parents are not paying sufficient attention to what their children are being exposed to and how well they are managing the challenges presented by such exposure. This lack of attention has resulted in some of the following unfortunate outcomes:

> *Eleven-year-old Josh was found in the school garage attempting to start a fire after suffering continuous bullying by his classmates; or Sophia, twelve, found at school in the girl's bathroom with her father's .22 pistol attempting to take her life after finding out she didn't make the soccer travel team; or sixteen-year-old Jean, hospitalized several times with an eating disorder and now she is cutting herself.*

The actions of these young people didn't reach the level of destruction like the rampage by Adam Lanza, the perpetrator of the Sandy Hook School shooting or that of Nikolas Cruz, who killed seventeen people at Marjory Stoneman Douglas High School. However, their emotional distress resulted in significant self-destructive patterns of behavior. Rather than lashing out at others, their feelings of helplessness, despair, anxiety, victimization, and sadness were turned on themselves. Yet what these children have in common with the perpetrators of those horrific events is a history of progressive warning signs that were recognized by some in passing. Unfortunately, not enough attention was devoted to actually addressing their patterns of behavior.

In each of these cases, parents were aware of the difficulties their children were experiencing. Some attempted to get help, but were inconsistent in their efforts; others refused to recognize the problem or else excused it. Even when the behaviors became more pronounced at home—falling grades, disrespect, angry outbursts, and self-isolation—the parents refused to respond to the escalating "emotional temperatures" as they progressed until it was, in some cases, too late.

These children aren't isolated examples. In fact they are more common than one might suspect.

Now before you stop reading and say, "You're not talking about my child. We don't have these problems. These are violent children, and I'm just looking for some parenting tips to help me clean up my family"— stick with me, we're going to get there.

First, recognize there are many factors that cause young people to have difficulties, impacting them and those they interact with. Family dysfunction, divorce—currently one out of two marriages end in divorce, with 60 percent of second marriages failing. One in fifty-nine children are diagnosed with autism; 28 percent of students in grades K–12 are bullied, with 43 percent of teens reporting that they're being or have been bullied online. Twenty percent of children aged thirteen to eighteen enter a classroom with an undiagnosed mental disorder, and more than three million children a year report being abused. In addition, genetic vulnerabilities, homelessness, technology, economic impact, lack of parental involvement, behavioral, academic, and social challenges, and many situations where parents just don't know or care enough or just need help— all of these factors impact their children's security, stability, and success.

Books, iPads, and Emotional Backpacks

Each day millions of children go to school with more than their books, pens, and iPads. They come with emotional backpacks often crammed with issues, concerns, and questions that influence and impact their daily success. Some enter school with healthy coping skills their parents helped develop. As a result, they make good decisions and progress academically, socially, and emotionally.

Too many others, however, come unprepared due to insufficient parental support, direction, and coping skills, and they manifest increasing negative responses and an inability to control their behavior. Such is the situation in the cases of Josh, Sophia, and Jean, who turned toward cutting, eating disorders, performance problems, isolation, and self-destructive behavior. Their heightened emotionality and inability to cope with their personal stressors led them into a progressive downward spiral demonstrating behaviors that sabotaged their success. What they had in common with the school shooters whose response trended toward violence was that their actions were visible to the significant people in their lives—if those significant people had been paying attention.

In school, these children are visible to teachers who themselves have little or no mental health training; these children act out, don't stay on task or pay attention or follow through on projects, have performance problems, are bullied, or are socially withdrawn. At home they may be nonresponsive, aggressive with siblings or friends, refuse to accept responsibility for their behavior, and fight with parents or spend hours online gaming, isolating themselves from their family and peers.

Unfortunately, today many parents aren't paying enough attention to what's really going on in their child's world. Overreacting, underreacting, or in denial, they make excuses for their child's behavior or are often just disinterested. Or they beg and negotiate with their children in a feeble attempt to get them to psychologically "buy into the right thing to do." In some cases, throwing money, gadgetries, and opportunity at them—

resulting in a self-indulgent child with a sense of entitlement and false sense of security, one that often blows up in the child's face once they enter adolescence and adulthood and find their behavior is far less excusable or accepted. Often these parents just need a new direction to parenting because in spite of their commitment, their results fall far from their efforts.

Many of today's twenty-first-century children don't have the skills to navigate through life's challenges, and when confronted with conflict or opportunity, respond with actions and choices they often regret, impacting their emotional well-being, performance, and future. But they don't have to, if parents pay attention.

Does it sound odd, telling parents to pay attention when the vast majority of us grew up having our parents tell us to pay attention? Yes, things have changed, mandating that parents recognize their child's emotional health, security, and success isn't automatic and can't be taken for granted. It's learned, and their responsibility as the most significant influencers in their child's life is to help develop it.

It's their responsibility to educate, support, direct, and influence their children toward choices in which their emotional well-being and responsiveness to challenges, disappointments, and successes can be effectively regulated toward positive outcomes.

A New Twist on an Old Theme

In 1825, Sir William Curtis, a British Parliament Member, dubbed the Lord Mayor of London, gave a toast at a Board of Education luncheon saluting "reading, 'riting and 'rithmetic." It wasn't known if he pronounced the words inaccurately or if he was trying to be ironic; the phrase stuck, and even today the three Rs are the basis for education.

The original three Rs focused on basic academic skills children needed to demonstrate proficiency in to succeed in and out of school. Those same three Rs are just as important today in achieving success, but not always that easy to master without help.

The New Three Rs: A Parenting Paradigm Shift

Today, success with the three Rs requires a different type of parental attention, one that focuses on developing those skills while also being aware of the constant influences and challenges affecting a child's performance, health, and safety in meeting those goals.

21st Century Parenting provides parents with a contemporary version of the three Rs. That is, three distinct and crucial ways in which parents need to pay attention. In this case the **Rs** stand for **Reading** (as in attending to what's going on in the child's internal and external world), **Regulating** (helping children cope and develop self-regulation), and **Redirecting** (guiding children to make good decisions leading to their success).

21st Century Parenting teaches parents to recognize those opportunities and the many challenges their children face. It provides a modern set of the three Rs with proven results leading to the development of successful, emotionally stable children with promising futures, who when confronted with conflict or disappointment, make decisions supporting positive outcomes, instilling a sense of confidence, control, and security that remains with them throughout their life.

- *Reading*

  Parents must pay attention to their child's world. Learning to **Read Their Child's Environment**, a parent comes to recognize the challenges, opportunities, and conflicts their children are presented with and who and what influences them, and how all of this affects their performance and success.

- *Regulating*

  It is up to parents to teach their children self-regulation. By recognizing the importance of **Regulating Their Child's Emotional Temperature**, teaching emotional control, parents can learn how children slip into negative mood states, and how if left uncontrolled such responses could impact their child's success—

coloring the decisions he makes, the behavior he demonstrates, and the responses he receives from his world.

- *Redirecting*

  Parents must learn to **Redirect Their Child's Behavior** in order to achieve positive outcomes, helping their child accomplish relevant goals that lead to a heightened sense of self-worth, self-assurance, and developing a balanced sense of drive for the rest of their lives.

So today there's a new set of three Rs, demanding parents pay attention to Reading, Regulating, and Redirecting their child's environment, emotions, and behavior, and in this way establishing present and lifelong success, emotional well-being, and motivation. Recognizing that what children might need is the committed leadership from the single most influential people in their lives: their parents.

CHAPTER 1

Reading Your Child's Environment

"It is easier to build strong children
than to repair broken men."
—Frederick Douglass

Each morning we get out of bed and sooner or later reach for technology be it our cell phone, iPad, or the laptop, then we turn them on and look for those bars indicating "power on." You see all green and now everything is right with the world because the world is at our fingertips. What's next? Google news, weather, directions, checking email, or any one of the thousand apps or more that provide us whatever information or convenience we're looking for to meet our particular needs. And of course it doesn't stop there. All day long we rely on technology to help us do something, get some place, communicate with someone, and to make us more efficient, more effective, and more successful, or not.

We check our stocks; how many steps we've taken; how many calories we've burned. There is an app for everything. Every aspect of our life, every part of our environment is being provided for, allegedly making our day, life, family, relationships, and business and financial world better. However, there is one major area that we cannot find on our smart phones—the one that informs us about the well-being of our children.

Wouldn't it be great for a parent if there was an app that could tell you how your child is doing and what to do about it? Today's technology can help us figure out where they are and, if we pay attention, what they've been up to. But what about what's going on in their world? What's influencing, threatening, and directing them? The things challenging them as they go through their day. Their safety; how they're performing academically, behaviorally, socially, and emotionally.

That app may be around the corner, but until it appears, parents need to be their own "parent app"—recognizing and responding to what's going on in their child's world. This is what I mean by *Reading Your Child's Environment*. Paying attention to what affects and influences them, to insure their safety and security and supporting their success as they develop through childhood, adolescence, and into adulthood.

But what does that world look like and what should a parent pay attention to?

- You begin by learning to read and recognize your child's world—the who, what, when, where, and how of it.
- Recognize that your child's world, like your own, is in constant motion and is constantly being bombarded by various influences in and outside of his or her control.
- Pay attention to those external influences that can lead children to make choices that are not in their best interests.
- Help your child navigate through the minefield of influences he or she is exposed to, identifying which are dangerous and which are opportunities for growth.

Growing up during the fifties and sixties in Southern California, there weren't many TV stations available to viewers. Programming began at 6:00 a.m. and shut down at 12:00 a.m. The programming consisted largely of various sitcoms, sporting events, and variety shows, all with commercials attempting to influence viewers both young and old. Fast-forward to today and things haven't changed much; however, now there are thousands of stations with twenty-four-hours-a-day programming and with far less control and regulation, all attempting to sell something to you and your children.

How do you compete with those marketing influences on your children, which are often contrary to your values and views? How do your children respond to such influences, and does that response impact their behavior or others in a positive way? The answer to these questions can have a profound effect on your child's daily life and illustrates why paying attention to what's going on in your child's environment is important.

> *In November 2015, a police sexting investigation began at a Colorado High School as a result of an anonymous caller contacting the Colorado's Safe2Tell Hotline. High school officials conducted meetings to inform parents that possibly hundreds of junior high and high school students may have been involved in the sexting scandal. An App called "Photo Vault" was the primary tool students utilized; a game where players engaged in exchanging hundreds of naked pictures of themselves online. Luckily, these students were let go with a stern warning from the legal community, and other than a football game being canceled and a number of students suspended, local officials chose not to prosecute. However, the potential for both short- and long-term impact to these children could have been devastating and carried serious felony charges; Colorado has a long-standing child pornography law that could have required those involved to register as a sex offender for the rest of their lives. In this case, parents and their children got lucky!*

Unfortunately, sexting among children and adolescents is all too common. What young people often don't realize is that posting or sending sexually explicit photographs or videos can impact them and have long-range consequences for years after a message is posted. This incident and thousands like it again support the rationale behind the need for parents to pay attention to what's going on in their child's world.

Bobby, seven years old, was escorted to the principal's office after he was discovered on the school playground drawing pictures of male and female genitalia. What his parents later found out was while being supervised by his nanny, the two would sit together at the dinner table while Bobby did homework and his babysitter watched porn. Obviously, Bobby found the programs his nanny was watching more interesting than his arithmetic. Mom and Dad: pay attention!

Core Development Competencies

So what should a parent pay attention to? Developmental experts identify various stages in an individual's life as milestones they develop through achieving success as they climb up their developmental ladder from childhood to adulthood. These stages focus on the various physical, social, cognitive, and emotional aspects of an individual's development. As a child grows from infancy through early childhood, adolescence, and adulthood, they work toward achieving success in these milestones mastering conflicts, challenges, and opportunities in their quest to maximize their future success. Working with thousands of children and families over the past two decades, Outreach Concern recognized a number of areas in addition to the developmental stages children are also known to experience. However, unlike the developmental stages they advance through, these areas are central and constants in an individual's life that mature as the child matures and must adjust to. We refer to these as an individuals Core Development Competencies (CDC). Similar to a child's developmental stages, these competencies present ongoing challenges and opportunities pertinent to an individual's life from childhood through adulthood.

A major goal for parents is to assist their children in adjusting to the various changes their Core Developmental Competencies and environment present, in this way supporting a healthy balance that ensures their safety, security, and success. Part of this process is developing both an awareness of the importance of these competencies and recognizing how crucial it is for parents to monitor and direct their children around and through the influences and conflicts they'll encounter as they develop toward adulthood.

Core Development Competency Domains

Health	How a child grows and develops physically and mentally
Family	How a child develops security and closeness
Behavior	How a child acts
Social	How a child connects with others
Emotion	How a child responds to challenges
Performance	How a child demonstrates success

As you can see in the chart, there are six Core Development Competency Domains that make up a child's developmental profile. Paying attention to each of these domains will provide you with crucial information relevant to your child's world, allowing you to be a more aware and effective parent.

Core Development Competencies are both independent *and* interdependent, in that they function with one another. Thus, the level of effectiveness in a specific competency can impact all of the others. If the deficiency or conflict in one area is significant, a snowball effect can occur that can lead to high levels of overall dysfunction and distress.

Chad is a sixteen-year-old sophomore, easy-going, sensitive, social, but highly self-critical. He gets in a fight with another student that results in his being suspended from school. The previous week he was involved in a minor automobile accident; a week prior, his girlfriend broke up with him. Chad's on the school baseball team and although he tries hard, his spends more time on the bench than on the field, which is difficult for him because of his commitment and love of the game.

In the midst of what looks like a series of bad luck situations, Chad's hospitalized with pneumonia and out of school another two weeks. During this time he is unable to keep up with his studies, and when he finally gets back on track, his parents find he's been failing four of his classes prior to being hospitalized—not turning in assignments, getting poor grades on tests, and lying to them about school.

A confrontation with his parents ensues over his failing grades prior to his other, more recent conflicts. Later that evening, his sister walks into his bedroom and finds him attempting to cut his wrists.

After Chad's suicide attempt, his parents attended counseling and reported that over the past several months he had become more isolated, not interacting with the family, spending more time in his room playing video games, and generally distancing himself from his family and friends. Even though they recognized these changes, they believed Chad would somehow "snap out of it," that his behavior was probably tied to just being a teenager.

Chad's situation exemplifies a young man demonstrating difficulties in almost all of the Core Developmental Competency domains described at the beginning of this chapter, affecting his health, family, safety, performance, and social and emotional life. His conflict in various competency areas collides with others, resulting in an overwhelmed and distraught teenager.

Even though Chad's parents were involved, they weren't paying enough, or effective, attention to what was going on in his life. This resulted in Chad's "emotional temperature" rising and falling like a roller-coaster due to his inability to cope with the losses and conflict he was experiencing. Eventually this led him to consider self-destructive alternatives.

How can you be sure there's not a "Chad" lurking in your family? By paying attention to what's going on in your child's world you can recognize whether or not your child is dealing with similar conflicts.

Therefore, a parent's responsibility is to recognize, anticipate, and direct their children through the challenges they encounter on their journey toward independence and self-reliance—ideally until they can operate independent of parental direction. Recognizing the importance of supporting a balance in a child's Core Developmental Competencies is the first step in that process.

Core Development Competencies are an important aspect of a child's development because they provide parents a picture of the world their children operate in, as well as helping parents identify the constant adjustments children experience throughout childhood, adolescence, and into adult life. The success or failure a child experiences in achieving a balance in these areas determines the extent of their overall health, welfare, and performance, leading to a well-adjusted child who embraces life's opportunities or a dependent, unfulfilled child who experiences a dissatisfied childhood and adolescence that carried forward into their experience as an adult. Familiarizing yourself with the Core Development Competencies provides you with a comprehensive profile of how your child experiences the world and gives you categories to focus on in supporting your child to successfully operate in that world.

Let's look at each of the Core Development Competencies in more depth. The following CDC examples provide parents an understanding of both the importance and the need for parents to be involved in their children's development and ways to go about monitoring their experiences. The examples also provide a projection of what a child might experience if parental intervention *isn't* incorporated to meet the influences and challenges they will encounter throughout their childhood, adolescence, and adult life.

CDC #1: Health Domain

A fifth grader, Maria, had recently been suspended from school for fighting. At school she had been a solid B student, never a behavioral problem, but had difficulty in making friends. Maria weighed 165 lbs. and was consistently bullied because of her weight; when she spoke to her mother about the problem she was told, "Maria, we're all big in our family and we love you just the way you are." Shortly afterward, Maria began complaining about stomach problems and refused to attend school. Her grades dropped; she began arguing with her siblings; a few weeks later, she ran away from home. Two days later, she was found in a park a few miles away with a twenty-eight-year-old homeless man.

Maria's parents were obviously not responding to a real need, which impacted her Health, Emotion, and Performance CDC domains. Although Maria's parents care for her, their response to her conflicts about her weight discounted Maria's feelings *and* her problem, which began to affect other areas of her life.

Like most kids, Maria wanted to be accepted, to establish enriching relationships and continue with the academic success she'd demonstrated. Yet instead of school being a positive experience where she was appreciated and accepted, it had become a place where she was ridiculed. Maria sought help. Her parents' refusal to recognize the legitimacy of her concerns, however, caused her to close down and act out aggressively—a way to protect herself from the pain she was experiencing. Her choices further sabotaged her school success and outlook for the future. Not only was Maria's physical well-being at risk, her school performance, social life, and behavior were affected by her parents' unwillingness to pay attention to her cry for help. Their discounting of her feelings resulted in an emotional-regulation conflict, leading to decisions that put her at further risk.

Okay, let's fast-forward and take a look at Maria. If her parents continue to discount her and not provide the support and direction she's requesting, what happens next? From a health standpoint, Maria's physical condition puts her at risk for diabetes, high blood pressure, and may even impact her life expectancy.

Maria's already demonstrating aggressive behavior at school, resulting in her being suspended, and she may feel she needs to demonstrate similar behavior to protect herself or position herself as an aggressive kid settling for negative attention. School is no longer a rewarding place for her, so the possibility of dropping out becomes a reality. She becomes at risk for substance abuse, self-harm, or suicide, as well as unhealthy relationships in her adolescence and adulthood. If Maria leaves school early, in spite of her past strong academic performance, it's unlikely she'll attend college or develop marketable skills that would result in a meaningful career; thus her economic success is affected.

Maria wants social acceptance from her peer group, who rejects her, and now even her parents minimize her feelings. Her reaction has been to pull further away from the environment she finds painful, as well as from her family, sabotaging the very thing she wants. Maria's circle of support dwindles and results in her looking for acceptance that she will possibly find in all the wrong places, further complicating her life. Mom and Dad, pay attention!

Maintaining your child's physical and emotional health and well-being is crucial. Questions parents should consider are: Is my child free from any physical or mental health impairment that could be impacting his or her behavior, performance, or competency? Is my child alert and responsive? Is he getting proper sleep, nourishment? Is there an eating disorder? Are there auditory or vision problems? Is my child physically healthy? Does she project a well-developed, physical and mental health presence in relationship to her age and maturity? Also, is he safe, is he making decisions that could impact his personal security?

How does a parent know the answers to those questions? Make sure your child gets a thorough physical each year, one that includes auditory and visual testing. Talk to your child's teacher. Is your child attentive in class, tired, or listless? Is your child on task, responsive?

Also, listen to your child's concerns. Don't minimize or provide a response that rejects or discounts his or her feelings. Your children telling you about how they feel needs your attention—it's their feeling about their experience, it's their reality every day.

Your child enters his world every day whether in school, on the playground, or in his society, competing with peers. The stress children experience in their lives—trying to fit in, to be included and a part of something, attempting to develop their identity—is no different than those experiences any adult would have in a similar situation. The difference is your child needs more help to cope and come up with answers that make him both be and feel healthy, and therefore he is dependent on you for his success. So make sure your child gets an A rating in the health domain, which means he is physically and mentally capable of performing at his best.

CDC # 2: Family Domain

Michael, a nine-year-old fourth-grader, hears a commotion in his parent's bedroom; he and his sister go to the doorway. Michael sees his parents fighting once again. There's pounding on the home's front door, Michael's mother screams, the door breaks open, the police handcuff Michael's father and take him to jail. This is the third time this month the police have been out. Michael and his sister are held by Child Protective Services and released in his grandmother's custody. The children haven't seen their father for three weeks as he's in jail awaiting trial for domestic violence.

Michael is observed on the playground walking around robotically. He no longer plays with other children and has been aggressive with his peers. He acts out in class and has a difficult time concentrating. He experiences reoccurring nightmares about his mother, has a difficult time sleeping, and cries when he's separated from his sister.

Michael and his sister's experience impacts their CDC domains of Family, Performance, Behavior, Social, and Emotion, further causing confusion with how and who to connect to and undercutting their confidence in their family's stability.

Domestic violence, family dysfunction, homelessness, divorce, and substance abuse all create difficulties for a child, leading him to question himself and his worth when the security he expects from his family is threatened. Such insecurities and inconsistencies from their parents cause children to question not only their worth but also who will take care of them, love them, and provide for their needs and safety.

So what happens to Michael as a result of the conflict he's experiencing in his Family domain? Without parental intervention, Michael will possibly continue to act out in the classroom or toward authority figures, impacting both his Behavior and Performance domain. He may also become aggressive with peers, impacting his Social domain.

Constantly being exposed to family dysfunction will cause him to be on an emotional roller-coaster, experiencing degrees of anxiety and stress that significantly affect how he feels about himself, possibly leading to depression, anxiety, lowered self-esteem, energy, and a lack of motivation toward opportunities. As Michael grows older, experiencing a continued lack of support and security from his family, his Emotion CDC domain is further impacted affecting his performance, possibly leading to turning toward more negative options such as substance abuse, dropping out of school, or engaging in further dangerous at-risk behavior.

Additionally, the more Michael is exposed to aggressive behavior or negative examples of how his parents treat one another, the higher the probability these will be learned behaviors Michael may demonstrate in relationships once he becomes an adult, possibly repeating a cycle of domestic violence and abuse.

Parents who present an unhealthy family environment cause their children to question their importance and security. These children experience fear and anxiety, concerns of abandonment, questioning what will happen to them next if one or both parents leave. Their reactions are often manifested in school and at home with poor grades, aggressive outbursts, inability to focus, poor school relations, depression, and guilt. Mom and Dad, pay attention!

How secure is your child in his Family CDC domain? What message is your child getting from his parents' behavior? How does your child feel about his place in the family? Ask yourself: does my child feel secure in the family? Do he feel loved, supported, and safe? Does the child feel a part of the family? Do family members pose a threat to the child's welfare? Does the family demonstrate a stable, warm, safe environment, or do they create a chaotic environment possibly causing the child additional fear and anxiety? How is this manifested in other areas of the child's world? How are *you* supporting a sense of family and relationship in your children?

Recognize that a family guided by the parents is the initial and most influential socializing agent to developing meaningful relationships in a child's life. Establishing strong meaningful family relationships—ones in which structure, commitment, support, self-discipline, love, and acknowledgment exist—sets the stage for the child to demonstrate these behaviors in his or her own relationships. The child who feels an integral part of a family is then capable of initiating and demonstrating similar behaviors throughout his or her lives in his or her individual, personal, business, and adult family relationships. So, Mom and Dad, pay attention!

CDC #3 Behavior Domain

Sixteen-year-old Mike lives with his mother and occasionally sees his father on weekends. He's had a history of poor school performance, is nonresponsive to rules, has been suspended from school several times, and had a few run-ins with the local police. His parents have been divorced for seven years and won't agree on how to deal with Mike's behavior. As a result of their inconsistency, Mike does what he wants. With no boundaries to focus him, he refuses to do his homework, and has failed his second semester of high school, which results in his having to make up six classes in summer school. Last week, Mike got caught with alcohol in the school parking lot, and now he is facing another school suspension; over the weekend, he wrecked his car for the second time.

Mike's out of control, at-risk behavior continues to escalate because his parents don't agree on rules and guidelines for expected behavior. Their lack of attention to Mike's history of irresponsibility cosigns his behavior, which then continues to escalate toward more unhealthy outcomes.

Mike's actions suggest he has no concern for his behavior or how it impacts others, and it puts him at further risk of dropping out of school, abusing alcohol or other drugs, and having more run-ins with the law. His lack of self-discipline in school and his lack of having any direction sabotage opportunities for him to be considered for college and thus limit his potential for the future. The behavior his parents demonstrate provides him a skewed picture of relationships as well as a poor example of parenting, which will possibly impact his own relationships he may have later in his life. Mom and Dad, pay attention! Consider Bob, who at thirty-two provides an example of what may lay ahead for Mike if he continues in these behaviors.

Bob's parents divorced before he was born, and he was raised by his mother. His father relocated out of state, relegating contact with his son to holidays and summer visits. Bob's mother, a highly supportive parent, had a tendency to overcompensate and make excuses for Bob's behavior, seldom placing demands or expectations on him for home or school performance, resulting in Bob becoming highly dependent and unaccomplished.

His father, remarried, had two children with his new family and demonstrated a stronger parental position, one with clear expectations regarding his children's performance. When Bob came to visit, he was expected—along with the other children—to follow through with chores and family responsibilities. This made a stark contrast to the life Bob led with his mother who put few expectations on him and also provided a supportive audience for his complaints regarding his father's "unjust treatment and expectations."

Around the time he turns twelve, Bob stops communicating with or visiting his dad. His school performance continues to be mediocre; he has few friends, is never involved in outside activities or sports, and fails to graduate. He has little interest in attending college. Over his early adult years, Bob holds a variety of part-time jobs but generally relies on his mother for support. He finds himself unsuccessful in personal relationships and continues to live at home, moving from one job to the next, often being fired for performance or attendance issues.

Mike and Bob's parents didn't pay attention to their sons' Behavior CDC development. Mike's behavioral issues were supported by parents who cosigned his noncompliant and irresponsible attitude and actions by their refusal to cooperate on a standard expectation for his behavior. Their lack of clear boundary setting, parental expectations, and consequences allowed Mike to demonstrate out-of-control behavior that impacted him and others.

In Bob's case, his parents' lack of cooperation throughout his childhood and adolescence, coupled with his mother's overcompensation and unwillingness to establish reasonable expectations for Bob's performance, supported his lifelong dependency on his mother, resulting in his failure to launch into adulthood successfully.

In both Mike and Bob's situations, the lack of parental direction toward their Behavior CDC success impacts their Performance, Social, Behavior, and Emotion domains, and this established an undisciplined approach toward opportunities. This leads to not only the various failures they're experiencing in the present but predicts a negative impact on how they embrace the inevitable life challenges they will encounter throughout their lives. A lifestyle of missed opportunities and lack of accomplishment will further affect their self-esteem, self-concept, and self-motivation. What's in store for their future?

Paying attention to the behavior your children demonstrate is about establishing the self-discipline they will need to develop and rely on throughout their lives. It should begin with these questions: Does my child follow the rules? Are there reasonable rules and boundaries that instill structure and parental expectations? Do my children understand what's expected at home, in school, and in society? Do they know how to treat their peers and siblings appropriately? Is their behavior impulsive and reactive, or timely and controlled? Do they get reinforced for the positive behavior they demonstrate or do they hear more *corrective* direction—constant comments on what they *aren't* doing? Are they open to feedback? How do they respond when they're corrected? Is their behavior and response age-appropriate? Does it invite the involvement of others or push them away?

CDC # 4 Social Domain

> *Julie's a fifth-grader brought up in the Midwest. Her family recently relocated to Southern California. She's entering a new school where all the children have been together since kindergarten. In her previous school, Julie had friends and was successful in her studies, on the soccer team, and was*

recognized as a great softball player. Beginning at the new school presents a number of challenges; making friends takes time, and one must get comfortable with new surroundings.

Sports were always Julie's support system, but unfortunately the family arrived too late in the season for her to get involved in any of the athletic programs at the new school. Having difficulty developing her Social CDC domain and not having the ability to use her athletic prowess to set the stage to develop more friends, Julie begins to come home complaining about not fitting in. She spends more time in her room, too, isolating from her family.

Julie's parents recognize the difficulty she is having but tend to minimize her situation, telling her it will just take time to meet new friends and everything will eventually work out with sports once she gets her opportunities on the teams next year. Still, Julie's grades started to drop, and her teachers report that she is showing little interest in school and isn't making friends. Then her parents discover she's started cutting as a means of dealing with the stress she's experiencing.

In spite of technology and social media, we still live in a social, interpersonally focused world. Being "liked" on Facebook by hundreds of "friends" will never take the place of feeling accepted by two or three "real friends" who you look forward to seeing every day. Having strong social relationships validates a child's importance. Friends are there to listen, to support, sometimes argue and fight with, but also to make up with—friends with whom to have play dates and sleepovers, who make one feel cared for, supported, and important.

Home and school are the testing grounds for these social connections in which a child learns to participate, to be a part of something, and to be accepted. Julie was on her way to developing a strong social world but she got detoured. Her parents were not paying sufficient attention to her difficulties and needs; they didn't provide the roadmap to get her back on track to the social success she had previously established for herself.

Julie's parents' response to her situation was a common one: "It will all work out, it just takes time to make new friends" discounts the importance of her Social CDC. They're paying attention, but not enough and not in the right way, and they need to recognize their responsibility in helping bridge her social gap, which broke down as a result of the family relocation.

In Julie's case, a new environment presents challenges and it's Mom and Dad's job to minimize the impact before these challenges become a crisis. Leaving a comfortable environment with established friendships causes Julie's emotional temperature to rise. Figuring out how she's going to be accepted and develop new friends becomes the most important thing on her mind. Having to start all over and get recognized is difficult and stressful. The stress of walking into a new classroom for the first time when everyone already knows each other is frightening enough, and even more so if a child doesn't have someone to help create that emotional safety net to help her establish confidence in her new environment.

Minimizing the importance of your children's social connections causes degrees of anxiety that significantly impact how your children feel about themselves and also their willingness to risk and initiate in other opportunities. Unless Julie's parents pay attention, she may continue to isolate herself, moving further away from the very relationships she wants to establish. Their lack of attention to her Social CDC domain will further impact her school performance, adding additional stress and causing her emotional temperature to continue to rise.

Now Julie has begun to cut herself in order to cope with the negative feelings she's experiencing. Because Julie's parents aren't responding, she's feeling more isolated from her family, the only real connection she has left. This may result in Julie distancing herself further from accomplishments that build her self-confidence making her more susceptible to influences that can negatively impact her health and welfare.

In Julie's situation, her parents could have helped by discussing openly what it was going to be like to start off in a new environment. They could have connected with her teachers and school counselors, creating a bridge from her former to her new environment.

In recognizing the challenges their daughter was going to experience with this new transition, Julie's parents could have minimized the loneliness, isolation, and anxiety she's experiencing, preparing her for the inevitable challenges and providing alternative responses to shorten the time frame in which Julie comfortably establishes her new social connections. Mom and Dad, pay attention!

Parents need to pay attention to how their children react in relation to their social community. Questions to ask: Is my child social, do they make friends easily? Do they make connections in school, initiate engagement, welcome others, maintain friendships? Do they demonstrate appropriate social skills that allow them to deal with conflict effectively, or are they alone, sullen, non-communicative, and aggressive and if so, what steps have I taken to help my child establish a position in his or her social world? Mom and Dad, recognize that if your child's Social CDCs are in conflict, a major part of his or her life is in conflict.

CDC # 5 Emotion Domain:

Cody is ten years of age and a great athlete—he plays soccer, basketball, and baseball. He is a friendly, open kid, popular at school; his grades are above average and he's got a great relationship with his parents and siblings. Cody's mother received a phone call from the school nurse informing her that her son was having stomach problems. Mom picks up Cody and he seems to be more comfortable when he gets home. When Saturday rolls around and Mom's ready to take him to the baseball field, he again complains about feeling sick. During the following week Cody reports a number of physical complaints he's experiencing, some of which interfere with his sleep. Cody's father, a fireman, addresses the problem with his son and decides to bring Cody in for a check-up. Cody's pediatrician gives him a clean bill of health, which eases his parents' minds, but the boy continues to complain when it's time to go to school or participate in the sporting events he enjoys. His grades begin to fall and there are more trips to the school nurse. Mom and Dad are concerned because Cody's healthy and nothing has changed in his life other than their once active, highly participative son is now sad and anxious. His parents notice this behavior seems to increase when Cody's father's not at home.

Mom and Dad seek some professional help. Cody's counselor discovers that several weeks ago, Cody had a sleepover with one of his friends. This young boy, unfortunately, lost his father a year before in an automobile accident. Like Cody's father, he worked the night shift, and he left for work one evening and, unfortunately, didn't return. The boy shared with Cody how difficult it was to never see his father again. Cody tells the counselor that if something like this could happen to his friend's father, he feared the possibility of the same thing happening to his own dad. This explained why the physical symptoms Cody described seem to only present themselves when Cody's father wasn't around.

Cody's parents were highly proactive. They realized, with the help of the counselor, the anxiety and stress that Cody is experiencing was coming from his belief the same outcome might befall his father and he would be in a similar situation to his friend. Cody's emotional CDC was adversely impacted, and it affected his school and athletics, performance, his ability to follow through with homework assignments, and started him toward isolating from his friends and other opportunities. His behavior made sense—if he stayed home with his dad, nothing would ever happen to him.

Cody's parents incorporated an aggressive approach to get him back to his former self. First, his parents spent time discussing Cody's concern, providing support and reassurance. Whenever possible, Cody's dad would drive or pick him up from school. He would leave notes in Cody's lunch box or school books as little "touch-base" opportunities during the day to remind Cody how important he was. He called Cody from work when he was on his break, Skyped with him whenever possible, and got Cody a cell phone with his dad's, mom's, and his grandparent's contact information, so when Cody began to feel anxious he could call them at any time. Of course, this was the first thing Cody tried, and for the first week or so he overdid it, until Mom and Dad sat down and discussed the overuse.

As Cody's parents supported this new approach, his emotional temperature declined. Cody got back to being the student, athlete, and social kid he was. As a result of Mom and Dad paying attention, they reversed the negative CDC snowball effect, resulting in their happy, active, emotionally stable son returning to his former self. Great job, Mom and Dad, for paying attention!

Fear, anxiety, sadness, and loneliness are all responses children commonly experience to changes in their lives, family, and environment they often don't understand and can't control. In the example of Cody, his emotional insecurities came as a result of a conversation between him and a friend. Sometimes a parent may not always be aware of a potential opportunity for this type of influence to present itself. So, obviously, paying attention to your child's emotional state is paramount. When a child's security and comfort zone are in jeopardy he can become overwhelmed emotionally.

Without having adequate coping mechanisms to deal with what life presents, the child's emotional temperatures rise and can sabotage his life. This is obviously what happened in Cody's case, and it can result in a variety of negative responses such as internalizing or externalizing the pain.

Parents need to constantly take their children's emotional temperature as it relates to their experiences, paying attention to how they regulate their responses to various experiences in their children's daily life. Some questions parents can pose are: Does my child feel and act in control? What does control look like? Are the responses she demonstrates to various experiences in her life reasonable? Does he manage and demonstrate a response appropriately? Is it reasonable in terms of the experience she is exposed to?

How does my child cope with disappointment or when things don't go his or her way? How does he celebrate success? Does she project her emotions on those around her, and how does that impact her situation or those she is exposed to? Does he make excuses for his behavior? Does she understand what an appropriate emotional response looks like, and can she demonstrate that?

What parents need to recognize is that they should be the model of what an appropriate emotional response is. Also, that they should teach their children to take responsibility for their emotional responses and become aware of how that reaction can impact others. Additionally, parents should try to provide resources for children so there is someone they can connect with when they feel out of control, hurt, angry, or sad, and to assist them in safely working through their negative emotions when parents may not be available.

CDC #6: The Performance Domain

> *Josh is a fourth-grader who has demonstrated academic challenges in most of his subjects from the time he entered*

school. He's nonresponsive to direction, doesn't stay on task, follow through, or complete assignments. Josh is constantly sent to the principal's office as a result of not following the rules or for being disrespectful to his teacher or other students. His parents have had numerous meetings with his teachers and the principal and finally agree to have Josh tested. He is diagnosed with Attention Deficit Hyperactivity Disorder (ADHD). Test results suggest a medical evaluation should be considered and that medication could possibly aid Josh in controlling his behavior, helping him to demonstrate more success in school and other areas. Yet his parents refuse to act on the recommendation and his performance and behavior continue to decline. Eventually Josh's parents stop returning the teacher's calls. Josh continues to do poorly in school academically and behaviorally, and now he fights with his parents about whether to go to school at all.

James is a quiet, unassertive third-grader. He seldom raises his hand in class or participates in group activities. At recess he's often found sitting alone on a bench, reading. James doesn't participate in sports, is lacking in social skills, and unfortunately has been bullied as a result of his reserved, passive behavior.

Both Josh and James have similar problems but demonstrate different symptoms, all of which support the same Performance CDC opportunities. Their behavior causes them to get negative attention, and their lack of accomplishments with academics and peer relations leads to their lowered self-esteem, confidence, and a sense of stagnation.

Josh is failing in school because his parents refuse to consider alternatives to provide support beyond what they've been able to provide. By turning their attention away from his behavior and lack of performance and by not responding to what the school's asking them to consider, continues to set up Josh for failure. A few more years of non-performance will cement Josh's belief that school is a painful place, one where he is unsuccessful and ridiculed. Why continue to be a part of something that makes you feel like a failure? The potential for school failure, early dropout, and drug or alcohol abuse places him further at risk.

James's CDC Performance issues may not be as overtly pronounced as Josh's. He quietly sits on the sidelines, frightened and anxious; he wants to be a part of his peer group, to fit in and be accepted, but doesn't know how. His parents are aware of his problem but unwilling to take steps to assist him in developing the skills that will allow him to be accepted by peers or to develop the assertiveness and independence to embrace opportunities where he can be successful. James is sitting on the sidelines because no one cares enough to help him get into the game. He's frightened to initiate or risk and doesn't have the skill sets to compete, so he's benched himself in the social game of life. He may not have the academic performance issues that Josh is experiencing but due to several years of not feeling accepted, his underdeveloped interpersonal performance will have a lasting effect on how he interacts with others for the rest of his life. For him there is the great potential to become more depressed or a larger target for being bullied or even becoming aggressive himself—turning his negative emotions on himself or others. His lack of participation sets him up for a drab, unhappy, unfulfilled existence.

Every child wants to be successful at home, in school, and in his or her social world. School and social performance is an opportunity to be recognized and to develop one's competency as well as a positive attitude toward healthy risk and challenge opportunities. Without parental intervention, children who have performance or learning challenges beyond their ability to control will experience ongoing failures. They see opportunities in school or with peers as nothing more than possible conflicts where they will be discounted and made to feel more incompetent. As an adult they don't take risks, and as a result, they fall further behind, come to question their ability and worth, and possibly suffer ridicule from others, all of which impacts the view they have of themselves. Mom and Dad pay attention!

School success and positive social and peer relationships are all about performance; they each lead to life success. Questions parents need to pose are: How successful is my child from a performance standpoint in school, socially, or when opportunities are presented? How does he respond in relationship to his readiness, willingness, and ability to perform as a student on the playground, in athletic endeavors, or his social society?

First a parent needs to find out what good performance looks like, and then consider how their child demonstrates and measures up. In the classroom, does the child respond to direction, complete assignments, feel good about being a student? Or is school a negative place where she experiences a lack of accomplishment because of her inability to perform? Does he participate in class, view school as an opportunity to be successful, enjoy being part of the learning process, progress to his highest degree of competency? Or is it a source of anguish, an experience that seems to get worse each day because he is impacted by issues beyond his control and needs parental support?

Performance issues in children aren't just to be regulated to academic success. Parents also need to investigate, support, and direct various areas in which performance may be a positive or negative challenge in other aspects of their children's lives.

Providing children opportunities both in and out of their school environment where they can learn and demonstrate performance success supports their independence, esteem, confidence, and motivation toward new challenges and opportunities both in their present and future careers. So, parents: pay attention!

This chapter has been about parents becoming effective at reading their children's environment; in particular, about paying attention to your child's Core Development Competencies and how to deal with issues and influences impacting your child's success and recognizing who he or she is going to connect with when experiencing conflict. This is the major role for moms and dads.

Paying close attention to a child's Core Development Competencies provides parents a daily road map to the levels of success or difficulty their children are experiencing with life's challenges; it helps illuminate what children need from their parents to help address the conflicts and detours impacting their success.

As parents, learn to pay attention to your child's world. Challenges and obstacles that conflict with a child's ability to create balance in his or her Core Developmental Competencies often lead to a rise in emotional temperature, further affecting a child's performance and personal competency. The following chapter addresses the second "R"—Regulating a Child's Emotional Temperature. A parent has the opportunity to teach their children emotional regulation, that is, to help them maintain emotional control with those growing challenges and opportunities they'll be exposed to throughout their lives.

CHAPTER 2

Regulating Your Child's Emotional Temperature

*"It's hard to think of anything that is more
socially beneficial than raising children well."*
—KERRY HEALEY

*Jack is a fifteen-year-old high school sophomore on the football
team. He was diagnosed with ADHD in elementary school
and his parents, after pursuing various options to help
improve his behavior and academics, finally incorporated
some medical management. Jack's parents want the best
for him and his sister and provide a reasonable amount
of direction, but are somewhat inconsistent with his
medication and have a tendency to view him as being more
capable of making independent decisions and following
through on school assignments without consistent reliance
on his medication or additional interventions than he is.
Unfortunately, they're often met with questionable results
and unwanted behaviors, and these throw Jack's father into
a tirade, which further upsets the family.*

*On Saturday, Jack approaches his parents with the request
to join some friends who are going to an amusement park later*

that evening. Mom is aware Jack has a number of missing math assignments, but agrees to let him go if he completes half of them before leaving. Jack agrees, and at about 7:00 p.m., leaves with his friends. Later, Mom's looking over Jack's work and sees none of the assignments have been completed. She immediately texts Jack, confronting him on not following through on their agreement, and the texting war begins. Jack insists he's completed all the assignments; his mother, of course, has evidence to prove otherwise. When Jack returns and is confronted by his mother and father about his dishonesty, he sticks by his story but can't produce the work. Finally, he shows his parents an assignment he did three weeks earlier, and the battle escalates with Jack becoming increasingly inappropriate, getting aggressive with his father, resulting in the police being called. The police calm things down and everyone goes to bed. Jack goes to school the next day and his parents immediately call the school and inform Jack's coach he no longer has permission to be on the football team. That night Jack doesn't come home from school, and he isn't found for two days.

When any or all of a child's Core Development Competencies are in conflict, his emotional temperature is affected, possibly impacting his logic, behavior, and response and, in many cases, how he acts and feels about himself and how he operates toward others.

As seen in this example, Jack and his family are experiencing multiple CDC issues stemming from Jack's learning and attention problem and his parent's inconsistency in their application of his medication and in providing leadership. His reaction and behavior affect the entire family, and as their emotional temperature escalates, they become equally out of control, further impacting Jack.

A major goal for parents is to teach their children emotional regulation in relationship to the various opportunities, challenges, and conflicts they experience within their CDCs. An opportunity that neither Jack nor his parents have achieved, resulting in the chaotic interaction the family demonstrates.

Developing emotional regulation needs to begin early in a child's life and, unfortunately, it is not automatic. Effective emotional control will follow children throughout their life and as such, needs direction and support in balancing appropriate responses to situations that can cause their emotional temperature to race up and down, impacting both themselves and those they interact with.

Early development of emotional regulation teaches a child to control and adjust his emotional temperature when exposed to various circumstances that challenge him, establishing a sense of readiness, willingness, and ability to risk, learn, and accomplish in various aspects of his life. Furthermore, developing effective emotional control early in a child's life establishes how he will deal with similar problems as an adolescent and adult.

> *Tim, a fourteen-year-old sophomore, is having a tough year. He recently moved from the East Coast, his parents are divorcing, his grades are slipping, and he's having difficulty making friends at the new school he's attending. One night, Tim posted the following to his Facebook page:*
>> *I have no friends.*
>> *I'm getting bad grades.*
>> *I have no talent.*
>> *I'm not good at sports.*
>> *I'm fat, I'm getting fatter.*
>> *I'm all flabby and out of shape.*
>> *I fail at life.*
>> *F*** MY LIFE. Someone kill me now!*

Tim feels he has no connection with his parents or friends. He is unhappy with his appearance and views himself as failing in various areas important in his life, which has resulted in him feeling helpless and out of control. Experiencing difficulties in multiple CDCs—the Family, Social, Health, and Emotion domains—is raising his emotional temperature to a fever pitch.

Emotional regulation addresses how an individual responds to various life experiences. Tim feels out of touch, disconnected, and unimportant to those around him. His answer is to stop his negative experience at any cost, and as his emotional temperature rises, his feelings of helplessness and failure cause him to question any purpose for his existence. If Tim's parents were paying attention to how out of balance his life is, they might intervene and focus on providing alternatives, assisting Tim in developing some success in those areas he feels he's failing in, helping him cope with his negative emotions.

As children develop toward adolescence and adulthood, their CDCs also mature as education, career, relationship, marriage, parent, and family situations present new challenges. Therefore, how they cope as adults within those more mature conflicts depends on how they learned to respond in their childhood. In Tim's case, his constant self-doubt, lack of confidence and accomplishments, and how he responded to them could result in similar responses he demonstrates as an adult—leading him to question his worth, ability, and significance.

In short, childhood and adolescence are the practice grounds for adulthood. Emotional regulation is needed to effectively deal with success and disappointment. Therefore, providing guidelines and support for a child's emotional regulation becomes the foundation on which ongoing and lifelong success and emotional well-being stands.

Children reaching adult status are often judged by their ability to juggle and regulate their emotions and responses to the various issues and circumstances as they are exposed to them. However, the adult society they enter is far less forgiving of an individual who can't demonstrate proper emotional control. If not confronted early in their development, the inability of an individual to control his emotions and demonstrate appropriate behavior at work, home, in relationships, and with his peers can negatively impact that individual's success, performance, and relationships for the rest of his life.

The solution is to help your child get it right the first time. You have eighteen years of trial and error, but it shouldn't take a child the entire time to perfect emotional control. The ultimate responsibility to helping your child establish emotional regulation and becoming effective in controlling his emotional temperature depends upon parental involvement, teaching, modeling, and providing corrective action. Early intervention establishes the foundation for successful emotional regulations and a sense of security for the rest of the child's life.

The primary model of how children learn to regulate their emotional temperature is what they observe in others. In particular, how their parents deal with difficulties that exacerbate their emotions. Your behavior, your reactions, and management of your emotional temperature is the first model teaching them how to regulate their own emotional temperature and response. So parents need to be aware of their behavior and how it affects others because their behavior is always presenting the primary examples for their children to follow.

> *Shawn and Mike are twins in fourth grade. Throughout the year they've been called into the principal's office regarding their aggressiveness and bullying of other students, and twice they have been suspended. Although the school counselor has brought their behavior to the attention of their parents, there has been little change in their behavior, which now has caused other parents to complain to the school principal. Shawn and Mike's parents show up for a meeting with the school principal and the boys' father immediately becomes defensive, stating he has no difficulty with his sons' behavior at home, doesn't see them as bullies, and that it must be the other children they are in school with. Further examples are provided regarding the boys' behavior, and Dad's voice gets louder and more*

threatening. The principal tries to calm the situation down, which only seems to incite more aggressive behavior on the part of the parent. When the principal suggests they set up a time for another meeting when all can deal with these issues with cooler heads, the parent aggressively refuses to leave the principal's office, which results in the school security guard being called to escort the parents off the school property.

In this situation it's not difficult to recognize where these two boys learned their behavior. The difficulty, however, is that they have no choice in terms of learning how to operate appropriately or not. The inappropriate behavior their father demonstrated, based on his inability to regulate his own emotional temperature, is passed on to each boy as appropriate behavior to demonstrate. Two months later the boys were asked to leave the school as a result of fighting with other students. Unfortunately, until their father recognizes that his behavior presents an inappropriate model, the boys will continue to have difficulties in school and with peers, and possibly the stage is set for difficulties throughout their lives—unless this behavior is addressed.

Along with being the most important models of appropriate emotional control, parents also need to recognize that the stress and challenges children experience in their daily lives are as significant as the adult stressors they experience in their own lives, but unlike adults, children don't always have access to the same coping mechanisms.

The day-to-day experience of going to school—performing in the classroom, on the playground, interacting with peers, being accepted or rejected, seeing how they measure up against others—is the stress your children live with in their society. Entering middle school, graduating, and going on to high school and then on to college—all produce major life changes and cause emotional temperatures to rise. Your child's ability to perform successfully in these situations relates to how she controls herself when confronted with those situations, which again is why early parental intervention is crucial. Parents need to recognize the stressors their children experience and create a supportive and ongoing dialogue on how to effectively deal with the challenges, successes, and disappointments their children experience daily.

That dialogue begins with establishing an atmosphere that both solicits and welcomes your children's willingness to share their experience without feeling judged or threatened. You can't minimize or discount their experience no matter how simple you feel it may be or that their feelings connected to it may sound—recognize its intensity from your child's point of view.

However, even when children have the tools to manage these situations effectively, with involved parents helping them develop and support emotional regulation, unexpected situations present themselves and impact a child's life, causing the child to react in ways that necessitate both parental and sometimes outside intervention.

A twelve-year-old in middle school, Laura, is social, described as a pleasure to have in the classroom, and yet announces she no longer wants to attend school. When her parents force her, a fight ensues. On those few days she does go to school, she's in the nurse's office asking to go home. At home, she gets along well with her siblings and parents, but no longer responds to friends when they call. Her mother reports her eating habits have also changed: she is shying away from her favorite foods, eating less, and this results in a trip to the doctor. Receiving a clean bill of health, her parents decide counseling may be an option.

What Laura and her counselor recognize is that several months ago she attended a birthday party. Laura described the party as fun—a bounce house, activities, pizza, hamburgers, ice cream—but when she returned home she started to complain about a stomachache and soon began throwing up violently, whereupon the babysitter contacted her parents.

Her parents immediately returned, and Laura eventually recovered. About two weeks later Laura started refusing to go to school, stopped seeing friends, and changed her eating habits. Later she shared that a classmate had gotten sick one afternoon, began throwing up, and other students made jokes about what happened. Laura explained she believed being sick at home could also happen at school as it had with her classmate, and she feared a similar reaction, with kids laughing and her being embarrassed. As a result, she determined she would no longer eat her favorite foods, which were the foods served at the party, and which in her mind caused her to be sick. If she could control that, she reasoned, the chances of her throwing up and embarrassing herself would disappear. However, the more she focused on what her classmate did, the more she believed this could happen at any time, and she concluded that her best course of action was to not go to school and to stop eating. A few weeks more with the counselor, and with the involvement of her parents and a good deal of reassurance, supporting the possibility that her fear being realized was unlikely, soon put Laura back on track. She returned to attending school regularly, went back to enjoying her favorite foods, improved her grades, and began interacting with her friends.

Laura's example points to an unexpected experience affecting multiple CDCs in her life due to her inability to control real and imaginative experiences, further influencing her response. Not having effective regulation tools caused her emotional temperature to rise, resulting in her fear of the possibility of having accidents at home and in school and experiencing embarrassment. This was further manifested in behaviors that eventually caused her to shut down, stuffing her emotions, becoming frightened, and projecting further failure in her mind that applied to anything she would try. Her actions led to behaviors, impacting performance problems, social issues, health, and the relationship with her family, which only furthered Laura's isolation and her fears about the future possibility of becoming sick and embarrassed.

Luckily, with the help of her parents and outside support, Laura was able to develop an understanding of her situation, which allowed her to gain emotional control, minimizing her fears. Now she is experiencing more success and self-confidence in her ability to control her health and opportunities as they arise.

However, a child who doesn't have the parental support Laura had may further isolate, not be open to change or opportunity, and become more reactive to her environment, diminishing her opportunity to achieve and accomplish, and impacting her personal integrity and success.

As a result of well-developed emotional regulations and the support of parental involvement, children who have control over their emotional temperature will be more relaxed and accepting with coping skills to assist them with the challenges they experience. They'll be more effective in demonstrating positive social relationships because they feel good enough about themselves to interact with others. They deal more effectively with conflict and disappointments as they have learned to recognize that one negative experience doesn't necessary lead to a lifetime of negative experiences. They feel comfortable expressing their emotions appropriately, understanding that anger, reassessment, excitement, and reinforcement are temporary feelings. They demonstrate consideration for others and view themselves in a positive light—even when experiencing a disappointment—and take responsibility for their own behavior. Overall, these children will demonstrate a positive attitude, performance, and behavior, which will result in their having consistent emotional success and heightened personal significance.

This is brought about by parents who are invested and pay attention and teach their child appropriate emotional regulation. These parents take note of the challenges their child experiences in his environment and direct him toward appropriate alternatives on how to deal effectively with conflict or confrontation. They observe, model, and demonstrate appropriate behavior, and they don't allow their child to develop and demonstrate responses outside his influence that could negatively impact his present and future behavior. And when their children do demonstrate such unhealthy behavior, they are there to direct them toward more positive responses.

A child who demonstrates positive emotional regulation demonstrates:

- The ability to cope with conflict and disappointment in a responsible manner.
- The ability to develop positive, social relationships.
- The ability to express emotion appropriately.
- The ability to demonstrate consideration for others.
- The ability to view him- or herself in a positive light.
- The ability to take responsibility for his or her behavior.
- The ability to demonstrate a positive attitude, performance, and behavior that results in his or her emotional success.
- The ability to recognize how his or her behavior impacts others.

The result of proper emotional regulation is successful performance and an increased sense of confidence stimulating similar responses and behavior before whatever other challenges a child is exposed to.

For a child who doesn't demonstrate appropriate emotional regulation, results are quite the opposite. When exposed to conflict they often feel out of control, which gives rise to negative emotional temperature and results in a child sometimes feeling alone, unappreciated, rejected, sad, depressed, overwhelmed, confused, and unsupported. Sometimes this leads to anger, rage, and possibly even aggressive or violent behavior, which can further impact how the child feels about him- or herself and how others may respond to him or her.

What does a lack of emotional regulation and rising negative emotional temperature look like?

- A child who stuffs his or her emotions.
- A child who can't accept responsibility.
- A child who demonstrates aggressive behavior toward others.
- A child who demonstrates unrealistic expectations.
- A child who can't see how his or her behavior impacts others.
- A child who has performance problems in school or at home.
- A child who can't deal with disappointment or loss.
- A child who isolates him- or herself.
- A child who is reactive.

Just as with positive emotional regulation, these reactions are learned, and unless parents intervene, they will grow and develop and lead eventually to negative consequences. From birth a child will be more reactive than proactive to his environment, as a result of everything being new and possibly frightening. Therefore, the foundation for emotional control rests on the parents to establish a safe, secure environment that projects and promotes emotional stability. A child who experiences family dysfunction, economic impact, social stress, learning disabilities, parental inconsistency, and undiagnosed and treated mental disorders are likely to experience increased difficulties in dealing with these issues due to feeling out of control. The child may demonstrate further unhealthy coping mechanisms by responding with threatening behavior, further impacting his health and welfare and possibly others in his life.

Without parental intervention, these responses can become exaggerated, increasing a child's emotional temperature. This results in lowered self-esteem (shame) and confidence (doubt), which negatively affects motivation toward new challenges and opportunities, present and future.

Ongoing parental direction and supervision establishes a child's ability to effectively cope with the surprises, conflicts, and opportunities life will present her, allowing her to achieve the results she desires. Her reaction to such conflicts will establish how she is accepted or rejected by those she interacts with: peers, siblings, parents, teachers, and bosses. It will also establish how she teaches her own children to demonstrate emotional control when she becomes a parent. Incorporating the following three steps will assist parents in developing and maintaining their child's emotional control in present situations and throughout his or her life into his or her future.

Three Steps to Positive Emotional Regulation

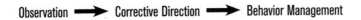

Observation ➡ Corrective Direction ➡ Behavior Management

Observation: Recognize the reactions, responses, and behaviors your child demonstrates to the situations he or she is exposed to.

Corrective Direction: Direct the change you want your child to demonstrate as well as your child's awareness and acceptance of their responsibility for their behavior and how it affects others.

Behavior Management: Supervise your child's behavioral changes and support the results they demonstrate.

Observation

Goal: Be on the lookout for examples of how your child deals with emotional situations. In observing your child's emotional control, recognize that it is sometimes difficult to be objective when addressing your own child's behavior. Therefore, pose the following question: How would my child's reaction and behavior be viewed by another?

- Is my child's reactive behavior appropriate?
- What kind of reaction does it produce: positive or negative?
- Can it impact my child's success both now and in the future?

- Is anyone else affected by my child's reaction?
- What response is generated by others as a result of the behavior my child is demonstrating?
- What does the reacted behavior look like, and how may it feel to others?
- Where is the response learned—from parents, siblings, peers, TV, internet, gaming, online? In other words, who's teaching my child to react in this way?
- What reaction have they received from others?

Corrective Direction

Goal: Your objective is to stop the inappropriate behavior and provide alternatives your child can demonstrate, as well as to get him or her to take ownership for his or her behavior. Immediately confront the behavior you see, but don't be critical or judgmental; be specific with an alternative and focus on the change you want to see demonstrated.

- Address the behavior you see.
- Identify the response you want.
- Give the behavior a name.
- Don't generalize or judge; be specific.
- Get the child to understand, acknowledge, and take ownership of his or her behavior.
- Explain how the behavior impacts others.
- Direct the child toward the alternative response you expect.

Behavior Management

Goal: Supervise and support the appropriate response you see your child demonstrate. Keeping the new response and behavior well oiled and running smoothly means paying constant attention and managing the behavior you expect.

- Observe and comment on your child's response.
- Provide ongoing corrective direction and support for the response you see.
- Closely manage what change you are requesting.
- Identify other's responses your child could incorporate.
- Ask how your child feels about the behavior he or she is demonstrating and the reaction he or she is seeing.

Reinforce the behavior you see, but only support demonstrated results. Make observation, correction, and management of emotional control a part of your family conversation. There are constant examples around your children, both appropriate and inappropriate, that demonstrate proper and inappropriate emotional control. You should be an ongoing director and model of what you expect.

Remember, in order for your child to develop proper emotional regulation, you have to live it as well, both in and outside your family. That means promoting and modeling positive emotional control, which will lead to your child's ongoing success in the various challenges your child will experience the rest of his or her life where emotional control is a societal expectation.

The two previous chapters have addressed the importance of Reading a Child's Environment—recognizing the world children live in today and the influences impacting their success—and how crucial it is to Regulate Their Emotional Temperature—recognizing the conflicts, success, and disappointments children are exposed to, and supporting their emotional stability and wellbeing.

The third R, Redirecting Your Child's Behavior, is about achieving success, personal competency, and significance. It presents parents a "Parenting GPS" vehicle that can help direct children to become self-reliant, strong performers who feel pride, assurance, and drive, leading to solid accomplishments and establishing a lifetime of success.

CHAPTER 3

Redirecting Your Child's Behavior: The Parenting GPS

*"Until you value yourself, you won't value
your time. Until you value your time,
you will not do anything with it."*
—M. Scott Peck

It's Saturday afternoon and parents are in the grandstands at the local Little League field introducing their Little Leaguers to America's national pastime. Two teams of eight-year-olds take the field. The majority of them are inexperienced and seem more impressed with their uniforms, the snack shack, and an occasional butterfly that drifts onto the field than they are with the game of baseball.

Bobby walks up to home plate for the first time, dragging a bat half his size. He stands at the plate and watches the first ball whoosh by. The umpire yells out, "Strike one!" Bobby looks up inquisitively at the umpire as his dad shouts, "Keep your eye on the ball, Bobby!"

The second ball comes whooshing in and someone from the stands yells "Swing!" and Bobby does, spinning full circle until he falls down. "Strike two!" the umpire cries.

Bobby stands up. Here comes the third pitch. Bobby swings. He makes contact with the ball, but stands still. The crowd yells for him to run. Bobby takes off running up the third baseline. Someone yells, "No, the other way!" and Bobby changes directions and charges to first base. The crowd applauds. Bobby grins.

A few innings later, Bobby approaches home plate for his second time at bat. There's a little swagger in his step this time, and he doesn't seem to need as much direction as he did before. In fact, Bobby almost looks like he knows what to do. He strikes out, but is definitely surer of himself at the plate than he was the first time.

Your kids face their "first time at bat" every day, with a stream of new challenges. This is a good thing! Every "first time at bat" is an opportunity for your child to develop self-esteem—even when they strike out.

After all, how many times does a kid hit a homer, get an A on a test, become captain of the football team, or get a job? Sure, the successes are wonderful, but what really matters is that your kids try, and try again. Through their attempts, they will begin to accumulate accomplishments, and establish their own sense of personal competency. It's the effort over time that increases their self-esteem, heightens their self-confidence, and gives them the motivation to try again.

Contrary to Popular Belief, Praise Does Not Create Self-Esteem

An unfortunate misperception among today's parents is that their children's lack of success or emotional instability is due to a lack of self-esteem. The belief has taken hold that constantly praising a child in an effort to build his or her self-esteem will magically lead to improved behavior.

The opposite is true. Of course you want to support and encourage your children and let them know they are loved no matter what. Just don't confuse that with building their self-esteem. A child has to work for self-esteem.

Yes, I said, "*Work* for self-esteem." To put it in very simple terms, you can praise your kid all you want. It will not help him learn to tie his shoes. But if he learns to tie his shoes, he's going to feel proud of his accomplishment. That sense of pride and accomplishment is what will build his self-esteem. It's his achievement of a result—all by himself—that builds his self-esteem.

Self-esteem is not a birthright any more than emotional control and self-regulation are. Self-esteem results from performance, experience, and accomplishment. Trying, doing, and achieving form the basis of how your children feel about themselves. Little accomplishments every day are what build the sense of pride, assurance, and drive you hope to see in them. In short, your kids can't feel good about themselves if they don't accomplish things.

You can't find self-esteem at Target on aisle nine. You can't see it, touch it, or taste it, but you sure know if your child has it or if she doesn't. There's no pill or quick fix for its development, but if not addressed, lack of self-esteem can affect your children throughout their lives, following them to adulthood and causing them to question their value and competency.

When kids avoid trying, they lose out on opportunities to develop their self-esteem. This leads children to question their own credibility and deteriorates how they feel about themselves. This in turn damages the motivation they need to try again.

A child who feels shame and develops a negative sense of self avoids new opportunities for accomplishment. This creates doubt and fear. This child starts to actively avoid opportunities to perform, which leads to stagnation and low motivation. This vicious circle can result in a passive approach toward future opportunities that may be demonstrated throughout an individual's life.

At Bobby's baseball game, in contrast, the accomplishment of hitting the ball created within him a sense of personal credibility. This stimulated his belief in himself and his willingness to return to the plate.

Accomplishments, however small they may seem, are what build a child's personal credibility; accomplishment establishes a foundation of confidence. It's your responsibility as a parent to create opportunities for your kids to accomplish and to direct and support their efforts.

Guiding Your Kids Toward Personal Significance

Achieving success in childhood, adolescence, and adulthood is a journey toward developing one's personal significance.

That's quite a mouthful! But what does it really mean?

The quest for personal significance lasts a lifetime, seeking along the way answers to these questions: Does my life matter? Why does my life matter? To whom does my life matter? Will my life have an impact on the world?

To help our children develop a sense of personal significance, we must teach them how to recognize and engage in meaningful activities in their lives where they can experience a sense of accomplishment. This is where the third R—Redirecting Your Child's Behavior—comes into play.

If we don't guide our kids in their quest for meaning in their lives, other—potentially dangerous—influences will step in that can impact their lives and possibly others' success, health, and welfare.

> *Bobby is seven years old and in the first grade. His parents have been asked to pick him up three out of the last five days of school due to his behavior, an ongoing problem since school began. Bobby hides under his desk, is aggressive with other children, and won't stay on task or respond to direction. His parents agree with this assessment and admit they see the*

same behavior at home, stating, "We talked to Bobby about his behavior, but it doesn't change."

Chloe is sixteen, a junior in high school. Her freshman and sophomore years were successful; she was maintaining a B average, had a great group of friends, and was on the soccer team. At the beginning of her junior year, Chloe began complaining about feeling anxious, was late in getting started for school, and then began missing days. She complained to her mother she was ill and too anxious to go to school. Her grades dropped, she stopped seeing her friends, and has now missed thirty-three of the last forty-five school days, putting her in jeopardy of failing the semester. Mom has taken her to a doctor, where she received a clean bill of health. Chloe still refuses to go to school and Mom feels powerless to get Chloe to change her behavior, which continues to decline.

Eighteen-year-old Jakob Wagner of Wisconsin opened fire outside the Antigo High School prom on Saturday night, April 2016, wounding two students; he was later shot and killed by authorities. As described by students who know him, Jacob was a "socially awkward kid who struggled to fit in and was bullied through junior high and high school.

From all indications, it seemed many people knew a lot about Jacob. All were witness to an unhappy kid evolving into a frustrated young adult, his manner of dealing with his disappointment resulting in this tragedy.

Yes, Jakob's case is extreme, but is an example of someone who's quest for personal significance, accomplishment, acceptance, and success was consistently unrecognized. Where were the important people in his life? Why wasn't someone paying attention, providing him direction?

Unfortunately, these young people represent everyday examples of millions of children who don't feel important. Bullied because they're different, humiliated because they're chosen last each day at recess, picked on because of their size or lack of ability, confused because of their identity. All looking for acceptance, all desiring to feel accomplished. Without parents focusing on redirecting their behavior, possibly like Jakob, their lives become a never-ending hunt for personal significance, questioning their worth for the rest of their lives or worse.

This is why the third R is often the most difficult for parents to embrace because it calls for more parental leadership. It requires parents to sometimes make tough, unpopular decisions regarding their expectations of their children. It means deciding what's more important: being your child's best friend or directing and supporting their actions toward successful outcomes, when a child's choices differ widely from what's in their best interest. And yes, oftentimes this leads to parent-child conflict, where parents need to become the major decision-maker. That decision presents a crucial question. Am I a parent because I have a child, or am I willing to parent because I'm taking responsibility for my child's security, safety, and future success?

The third R is difficult because it requires action, commitment, reaction, and responsiveness. Because it's about your most important investment: your child's present welfare and future success. Yes, *your investment*, and making sure you get the best possible return on that investment. Today, according to the Department of Agriculture, it cost middle income parents approximately $233,610 to raise a child from birth to seventeen years of age. That's an investment. The question is what type of return are you expecting? Unlike stocks, bonds, and real estate, where you can't control the variables affecting your return, you're the family CEO. You can guarantee your return if you closely monitor, direct, and support the outcomes you lead your child toward. In short, the third R requires parents to be leaders. You can become friends later, and your children will thank you for it when they're mature enough to understand your actions.

The first step in helping your kids develop personal significance is to help them develop a sense of personal competency. Think about how proud you were when you finally learned to tie your shoes; that fed into your sense of personal competency. Achievements within a child's CDCs establish their sense of personal competency. The resulting pride, self-assurance, and drive support an individual's efforts over his or her lifetime to develop personal significance.

What does a child with a strong sense of personal competency look like? She takes initiative; she's assertive; she will raise her hand in class, volunteer, take risks, sometimes fail, of course, yet be willing to try again. Children with strong personal competency don't let disappointments cause them to quit. They look up and out into their world. They participate, accept responsibility, and welcome opportunities to add to their accomplishments.

What about kids who don't have a well-developed sense of personal competency? They feel insignificant. They look down at the ground. They hide and don't take risks or initiate or volunteer. They're frightened, don't try, and they are often the last to be selected to join a team or some other group because they haven't developed the skills to impress themselves or others. They don't achieve anything because they don't know how. They don't believe that they can. They make excuses to avoid trying, or they overcompensate by pretending they have an expertise they can't backup with results.

Children who have not developed their sense of personal competency tend to shy away from opportunity and responsibility because of this lack of accomplishment. This can establish a pattern of self-doubt that will haunt them for the rest of their lives.

How to Redirect When Your Kids Get Thrown Off Course—and They Will!

Even kids with healthy self-esteem can get thrown out of whack. That's when parents need to step in with the third R of the three Rs: *Redirect*. Here's an example:

> *Eleven-year-old Sam is a likable kid. He makes friends*
> *easily, gets good grades, and has a great relationship with*

his parents. Both his teachers and parents praise him for his commitment to school. Sam also loves sports. When he's not playing baseball or surfing, he's on his skateboard.

Sam persuades his parents to enroll him in a summer skateboard camp. He's excited and happy when they drop him off at the camp, where he joins around 100 other young skateboard enthusiasts. But six hours later, unfortunately, Sam's parents get a call informing them that their son has broken his leg.

Sam returns home in a cast that he must keep on for weeks, making the rest of his summer vacation pretty miserable. While his friends are at the beach or the skate park, Sam is sitting on the couch playing video games, watching TV, and eating.

By the time summer is over and the cast comes off, Sam has gained nineteen pounds. He goes out for the school surf team, but is upset to find he doesn't have the stamina to make the team.

A month into the school year, Sam's parents get a call from his PE teacher saying that Sam's having a difficult time keeping up with the rest of his class. Sam has also been shying away from his friends, particularly if he is invited to go to the beach or to a swim party. He continues to do well in school, but spends more time indoors eating and playing video games.

Sam's parents have read the changes in his environment and have attempted to help him regulate his emotions, but to no avail. They recognize that Sam is unhappy and is losing his motivation and sociable nature. It's time to redirect his behavior. First, they sit Sam down and discuss his weight—a difficult conversation to have. They take Sam for a physical and meet with his doctor about a weight loss plan.

Mom and Dad decide to eliminate junk food and plan healthier meals at home, and to get the entire family to be more active. Sam reluctantly starts running with his dad each night. Three weeks into the plan, Sam is losing weight. He's enjoying running with his dad, and the entire family has embraced a healthy diet and exercising. Three months later, nineteen pounds are gone, and Sam is back to his old self. He's active, healthy, interacting with his friends, and in great shape.

Sam's accident affected his Health CDC and damaged the way he viewed himself. He became socially withdrawn and unhappy with his situation. This gnawed into his feelings of a lack of personal competency and personal insignificance.

Sam's parents read the changes in his environment, noticed that his emotional temperature was no longer well regulated and moved into redirecting mode. They made some changes on his behalf that initially Sam wasn't excited about, but eventually embraced because he saw positive results. This plan not only improved his physical appearance but also restored his ability to get back to sports and resume building his personal competency. The result is a kid who feels better about himself and is motivated to resume his journey toward personal significance.

As Sam's situation exemplifies, challenges will pop up as your child develops. Some challenges may seem overwhelming. That's when you need to step in to redirect his or her behavior in a positive direction.

Parental Leadership in Action

When you support your children in embracing opportunities and challenges, you set them up for success. You want to stimulate healthy risk-taking. This leads your kids toward personal assurance and motivation and away from the shame, doubt, and stagnation that result from lack of accomplishment.

Easier said than done, right? Some young people require more direction than others. This is where parental leadership comes into play.

The following diagram illustrates how a child's accomplishments establish a heightened or lowered sense of personal significance.

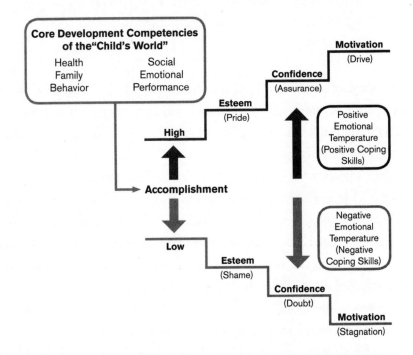

The central themes of a child's life are illustrated by the six core development competencies in this chart—Health, Family, Behavior, Social, Emotional, and Performance. At every step along the way you will need to provide your kids with direction, guidance, and support in each of these. As the next example illustrates, your parental leadership is still needed even once your kids head to college.

> *Eighteen-year-old Mattie recently graduated from high school and is in her first semester of college on a softball scholarship. Mattie embraces college life: she has joined*

a sorority and is enjoying the independence of being on her own.

Unfortunately, however, Mattie begins to have a difficult time balancing her class schedule and schoolwork with softball and her social life, and her grades begin to fall off. Her parents are in the dark; in the rare times when they do manage to get her on the phone, she tells them "everything is great."

Midway into the first semester, Mattie suffers an injury at softball practice that benches her for the season. The team's doctor gives her prescription pain medication, which Mattie begins to abuse, developing an addiction to Oxycontin. When her treatment ends and the prescription runs out, she begins selling drugs to feed her own habit. Her attendance at school begins to suffer along with her grades. Mattie fails her first semester and is put on academic probation. Her parents have no idea any of this is happening.

As the second semester starts, Mattie's drug business is far more successful than her school career. Halfway through the second semester, she and her friends are arrested for drug possession. Mattie fails her second semester, too; she loses her scholarship and is expelled. Mattie returns home, with her parents still completely unaware of what's going on in her life. She's lost a considerable amount of weight and becomes agitated when they press her about her issues at college. As her parents catch her in lie after lie, they finally recognize that their daughter has a serious problem.

Mattie's world is crashing down around her. She is demonstrating problems in all six CDCs and is suffering from loss of self-esteem due to her failure in college. She's saddled with a life-threatening addiction, as well.

Luckily, her parents begin to get more involved as soon as they understand she needs help. They get her into rehab, help her tackle her legal problems, and work with a therapist to support her recovery and get her back on track.

After rehab and counseling, Mattie gets a part-time job and enters community college. She is still living at home and is allowing her parents to monitor and support her in the changes she is making in her life. Over time, with her parents leading and supporting her, Mattie is able to increase her confidence, self-esteem, and motivation.

One year later, Mattie has completed two semesters of community college, maintaining a 3.50 grade point average. She is drug-free, has a great relationship with her family, and is playing softball again. These accomplishments are stimulating the pride, assurance, and drive she needs to stay drug-free and continue to succeed.

Mattie initially lied to her parents and resisted their efforts to read her environment, regulate her emotional temperature, and redirect her. Luckily, she eventually recognized that she needed their parental leadership in order to get out of the mess she had created.

Recognize that as a parent you have the right to redirect your child toward success. Sometimes their actions complicate that process, and sometimes they may fight you tooth and nail, but in the end, they will thank you for it.

Here's a diagram that shows how the process of redirecting your child toward personal competency and significance becomes a synergistic, self-sustaining process. You can apply this principle no matter the age of your child, and no matter what challenges he or she is facing.

Redirecting Your Child Toward Competency and Personal Significance

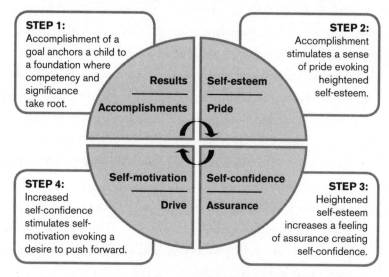

STEP 1:
Accomplishment of a goal anchors a child to a foundation where competency and significance take root.

Results
—
Accomplishments

Self-esteem
—
Pride

STEP 2:
Accomplishment stimulates a sense of pride evoking heightened self-esteem.

Self-motivation
—
Drive

Self-confidence
—
Assurance

STEP 4:
Increased self-confidence stimulates self-motivation evoking a desire to push forward.

STEP 3:
Heightened self-esteem increases a feeling of assurance creating self-confidence.

This synergistic process becomes self-sustaining, driving a child toward success and the ability to transfer their assertiveness to other opportunities.

ACCOMPLISHMENT → SELF-ESTEEM →
SELF-CONFIDENCE → SELF-MOTIVATION

"NOT AUTOMATIC, MUST BE DIRECTED BY PARENTS"

The key to remember is that none of the processes illustrated are automatic. They happen because they are stimulated and directed by parents who take a strong leadership position in the family.

The "Parenting GPS"

Have you been asking yourself, "Why isn't my child accomplished?" Consider reframing the question as "Why am I allowing my child to feel unaccomplished? Is it due to my lack of parental leadership and involvement?"

I don't say this to give you a guilt trip. Children can present widely varying attitudes and degrees of commitment toward accomplishing expected tasks and behaviors. The road to your kids becoming accomplished can be bumpy and impaired by "readiness, willingness, and ability" roadblocks. Parents need a "Parenting GPS" to help them navigate through the "responsiveness detours" their children demonstrate and redirect their kids toward a destination of success.

A child who is unaccomplished will not recognize the value of an accomplishment or understand the rationale for committing to trying. That's where parental direction comes in. The parent, not the child, must choose what's in the child's best interest until the child's responsiveness, responsibility, and results demonstrate his or her ability to self-manage and produce achievement.

The Parenting GPS diagram is a great tool you can use to figure out how best to redirect and motivate your child. It will help you identify your child's responsiveness toward your expectations, as well as the corresponding parental direction that is needed.

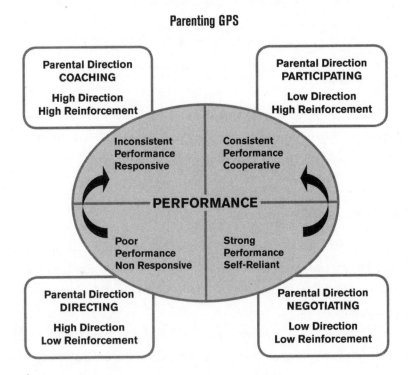

Parenting GPS

To use the Parenting GPS diagram, begin by using the performance circle to identify the level of performance and responsiveness your child demonstrates. Once you've identified those, then you can choose one of the four directional approaches: Directing, Negotiating, Participating, or Coaching. These are each designed to address your child's particular level of responsiveness.

By consistently applying this process, you can elevate a nonresponsive, poor performing child to a consistent, cooperative performer—one who is self-reliant, responsible, and participating.

Here are the four positions you can use at various times, depending on the corresponding behavior your child is demonstrating:

- **Directing:** A child who is nonresponsive and a poor performer needs parents to provide clear and specific direction for expected results, with minimal degrees of reinforcement until the expected change in behavior is visible.

- **Coaching:** A child whose behavior is inconsistent, but responsive, needs parents who operate like a coach, providing specific direction for expected results, as well as equal amounts of reinforcement for the results and behavior they see their child demonstrate.

- **Participating:** For a child who's a consistent performer and cooperative, a parent can be more participatory. Here, less direction is needed because the child demonstrates, in most cases, expected behavior. The parent acts as a supportive guide and is highly reinforcing of the behavior and results the child produces.

- **Negotiating:** For a child who's a strong, self-reliant performer, the parent's job is to negotiate and delegate opportunities. The child, in most cases, demonstrates expected behavior, and therefore the parent can provide less direction and reinforcement.

The rest of this chapter provides some real-world examples of the Parenting GPS in action. These examples are about children who are struggling and who demonstrate a wide range of responsiveness. In each case, parents were able to use the Parenting GPS concept to redirect their children and get them back on a healthy, happy track.

When Negotiating Fails

Sean, a fourteen-year-old freshman, is constantly frustrating his parents with his poor performance and lack of motivation. He began his first semester of high school strong, but ended up with two Fs and three Ds. Midway through his second semester, he's failing all his classes.

Sean and his parents have always gotten along well. They consistently discuss his extracurricular sport activities, as well as his academic performance. When it comes to grades, Sean promises his commitment to pay more attention in class, do his homework, meet with his tutors, and put more time into his studies. Conversations with his parents always end on a positive note, with Sean reassuring his parents his efforts and results will improve. His parents continue to reinforce his commitment, supporting their belief in him and his potential. However, the expected results are never demonstrated.

Why isn't Sean responding? What are his parents doing wrong?

First, Sean's parents are assuming something not in evidence, that is, Sean wants to change his behavior. He may actually want better grades, but what is he willing to invest to achieve those results? So far, he hasn't done much more than talk.

Sean's parents have failed to read Sean's environment accurately. He's in high school now and enjoying new freedoms, friends, activities, and a social life. As a result, Sean is having difficulty balancing his social life with his classwork, which has been taking a back seat in his school experience.

It's not that Sean is incapable of improving his performance; it's that his options have increased and his priorities have changed. As is the case for many newly minted teenagers, Sean's freedom and independence are now more important than putting time and effort into school to produce the results his parents expect. He views his social opportunities as having more value than his grades. He doesn't recognize that failing in school could have a negative impact on his future—and his social life.

If you look at the Parental GPS chart, you can see that the negotiating mode only works with kids who are already strong performers. Even though their efforts consistently fail, Sean's parents keep negotiating, and the revolving door of support, promises, failure, and parental frustration keeps turning.

Sean is putting on a good face but his poor performance in school is already eroding his esteem and motivation. Sean's continued failure is keeping him from experiencing accomplishments, and this is impacting his confidence, leading to further erosion of motivation.

One problem is that Sean's parents are responding to him as someone who is concerned about his performance. They misread his intentions regarding his commitment and continue to be highly reinforcing. They believe Sean will "psychologically buy into the right thing to do" if they keep reinforcing their belief in his potential, even though he has failed to demonstrate it.

Sean's parents need to shift into Directing mode. They need to demonstrate a controlled, take-charge approach to his performance. They need to direct his actions, police his behavior, schedule his homework, speak to his teachers and tutors, review his homework, mandate weekly progress reports, and close the door on his independence, which has provided him too much freedom to make poor choices.

Initially, Sean is going to be angry and resentful at what he'll view as his parent's overly severe interference. Up to this point, Sean has had things his way; his parents have taught him to view his situation as negotiable, and he has had a voice regarding the choices in his life.

Sean is not genuinely interested in negotiating, however. He has shown that he is only interested in making false promises that keep his parents off his back. That's why his parents need to incorporate the Directing approach. They need to control and direct his behavior until Sean improves his performance.

Sean's parents realized that the amount of time he was investing in his studies was minimal. As they moved into Directing mode, they provided higher degrees of direction for his schoolwork and lowered amounts of unearned reinforcement. Instead of engaging Sean in discussions and negotiations, they made their expectations clear and backed those up with action.

Although Sean was angry at first when his parents took away much of his newfound independence and began directing his academic life more rigorously, he became more cooperative as his academic performance improved and he began to earn back some freedom.

At that point, his parents used the Parental GPS to move into Coaching mode. Today, they operate more as coaches in his life—policing his actions, but supporting him for the results he demonstrates. Sean now demonstrates more emotional control regarding his actions. His new academic, behavioral, and emotional accomplishments have raised his self-esteem, confidence, and motivation to continue his success.

Coaching a College Student Who Has Moved Back Home

Megan is a nineteen-year-old college student. After graduating from high school, her parents sent her to a private school in Northern California, where she intended to major in fashion design. After doing poorly in her past two semesters, Megan moved home. Currently she is not attending school, is unemployed, and totally dependent on her parents. Megan's parents are disappointed with her poor results in school. They are distressed by her lack of motivation, the late hours she keeps, her unwillingness to get a job, the small amount of time spent at home, and her utter lack of plans for the future.

Frustrated, her parents demand that she either enter counseling or they will force her to leave home. Megan responds well to the counselor; she is open and communicative, and demonstrates little resistance. She tells the counselor that during high school she did poorly, underwent testing, and was diagnosed as ADHD. She was on medication for a short time, but chose to discontinue it because she didn't like how it made her feel. Additionally, her parents never pushed her to continue the medication.

Megan describes her family as close but interfering, "wanting to control her life." She explains that going away to college was exciting at first, but soon it became overwhelming and she just stopped attending classes. She made a lot of friends and partied a great deal, experimenting with drugs. She attempted a second semester, but her commitment and results were similar to her first. She had no place else to go and so returned home. Since that time, she has been supported by her parents.

Megan tells the counselor that she wants to leave home, but has no means of supporting herself and feels helpless to change her situation.

Megan is experiencing difficulties in her Performance, Family, Emotion, and Health CDCs and these are negatively affecting her confidence and motivation. These problems are elevating her emotional temperature, leading her to sleep in and avoid trying to get a job or plan for the future in order to try to avoid feeling worse. Megan had long tended to put in the minimal effort required to get by.

Because Megan is being fairly honest and wants to do better, the Parental GPS indicates that the Coaching approach could work for her. Her parents begin to incorporate this approach, recognizing that she doesn't need to be overly controlled. Her problem is consistency and follow-through.

Megan's parents begin providing clear specifics for what is expected of her, along with equal amounts of direction and reinforcement for what they see Megan demonstrate. By paying close attention to Megan's behavior, they get her to see that in her current situation, her choices are very limited. Her parents make it clear that they will not continue to support her without her taking action to get back on her feet.

With her parents acting as her coaches, Megan agrees to go through an educational assessment process. Testing reveals another learning disability in addition to her previously addressed ADHD, and a new medication is prescribed. Megan begins the medical regimen and her mother agrees to assist in temporarily monitoring it.

Next, the counselor and Megan look into taking classes at the local community college. Megan qualifies for some special assistance through the college's educational service and she enrolls in three classes for the new semester. She also agrees to look for a part-time job and is hired as a waitress at a local restaurant, which proves to be a rewarding experience. She develops a great relationship with the owner, who consistently reinforces her with praise and support for her commitment and performance.

Megan's parents continue to take a hard line monitoring her efforts, but are equally supportive regarding the results they see her demonstrate. They make her pay for school for the time being, but agree that should she receive Cs or better, they will reimburse her for school expenses. They agree that if she continues community college for two years and increases the number of classes, maintaining Cs or better, they will send her back to a university and pay her expenses there. They also require that Megan stay in counseling, continue seeing the psychiatrist, take her medication, and work for at least twenty hours per week employment. Megan agrees to their terms and eventually begins to feel more accomplished, which in turn fuels her self-esteem and motivation to continue.

Helping an Overachiever Who Is Burning Out

A sixteen-year-old high school student, Claudia is having unexpected emotional outbursts both at home and in school. Claudia has a 3.50 grade point average and a history of being an excellent student. She is involved in numerous school activities, has a part-time job at a local yogurt shop, babysits for neighbors during the week, and is on the school volleyball, track, and cross-country teams. She even volunteers at the local senior center, playing cello. Claudia has a great relationship with her parents, but her outbursts are puzzling them.

Claudia asks her parents if she can see a counselor. She explains that she's been feeling overwhelmed and frustrated and has been frightened about the possibility of failing this semester, which would destroy her chances for college.

Claudia's teachers all share positive feedback with the counselor and Claudia's parents, confirming her high marks and viewing her as a pleasure to have in class. Claudia denies any drug use. There is no history of anxiety or depression in her family. Other than experiencing insomnia lately, she is healthy.

Claudia has always been open, communicative, and highly involved with her family. She never had to be reminded to follow through on her chores or her homework, and she always got along with her siblings. Her parents' biggest concern was Claudia's tendency to take on too many responsibilities and overextend herself. When they addressed this with her, however, she dismissed their comments. Yet over the last few weeks, Claudia has been overly emotional at home. She is short with her parents and siblings, and on more than one occasion, has gone to the school nurse complaining of stomach problems.

Recently Claudia enrolled in the SAT study program, offered for three hours on Tuesday and all day Saturday. Claudia had also begun taking driver's ed. She got her license, and one of the team sports in which she is involved is going to the state championship, which requires additional practices.

Clearly, Claudia's plate is overflowing, but she isn't willing to see it that way. Because she values all her responsibilities equally, eliminating any of them makes her feel like she is failing both herself and the people who are counting on her.

Claudia's parents recognized she was highly cooperative, so they used the Participating approach recommended by the Parental GPS. Claudia doesn't need directions; she needs guidance and support. Claudia shows up, knows what to do, and is a responsible and cooperative performer. She recognizes when she has difficulties dealing with her environment and can sometimes come up with the answer herself. What she needs from her parents is support and reassurance that she's making the right decisions.

First, Claudia and her parents made a list of all her responsibilities. Next, they prioritized them based on the degree of importance they really had in her life. Together, Claudia and her parents worked out a new, lighter schedule that still enabled Claudia to continue to participate in most of her duties and commitments. This schedule allowed for time off from her job and reduced her babysitting schedule, which gave her some desperately needed time to study for the SAT and prepare for the state championship.

Support and minor directions from her parents helped Claudia to develop more realistic expectations about what she could do. This assisted her in organizing her day and controlling her emotions. She was able to get back on track without further insomnia and outbursts and move forward with her accomplishments, raising her self-esteem and motivation to continue to be as successful as she had been in the past.

Dealing with "The Arguer"

Mike is fifteen years old, an only child, and recently completed his first year of high school with excellent grades, similar to his past school experience. Mike has been complaining for some time, though, about being unchallenged and bored in school. As a result, his parents have enrolled him in a new high school his sophomore year.

Because Mike began the new school midway into his first semester, the school gave him the opportunity to enroll in regular classes versus the Advanced Placement (AP) classes he usually took. Mike refused, saying he would have no problem catching up and maintaining his grades in the AP classes. He also decided to try out for the lacrosse team, and made it. A few weeks into practice however, he quit, complaining about the coach and other teammates.

Mike's parents referred him to counseling because he was refusing to get up in the morning and go to school, complaining about stomach pains, and had emotional outbursts, lying on the ground holding his stomach.

Mike was adamant about not wanting to see a counselor, fighting with his parents over the idea, but he finally agreed. The counselor spoke with Mike's parents. They viewed their son as highly successful and college-bound, but had a tendency to make excuses for his behavior. They agreed to get Mike a physical, which resulted in a clean bill of health.

The review of Mike's records indicated a student who was a strong performer that maintained excellent marks.

Mike's teachers identified him as bright and competent, somewhat of a loner, and often argumentative. Mike also demonstrated difficulties with other students when he had to work on team projects. His former coach said that Mike had the potential to be a good athlete, but he would seldom show up for practice and had a difficult time taking direction. Throughout his life, Mike had tried out for a number of sports and made the team, only to quit eventually, complaining of difficulties with teammates or about what he considered the coach's unfairness.

Mike is a highly results-oriented individual, a competent kid who wants to do things his way. He shies away from group involvement and has a tendency to blame others for his own shortcomings. Because kids like Mike are seldom open to taking specific direction, employing a more indirect Negotiating approach often works best.

The goal here is to get Mike on board without demanding compliance, which would trigger him to fight his parents. In order to be more effective, they must recognize that Mike needs to feel respected before he will open himself to feedback or suggestions. Another goal is for his parents to help him feel valued and that he has some power in decision-making. His parents achieve this by discussing and negotiating his behavior, instead of controlling or finding fault with it.

Once Mike's tendency to fight was calmed, his parents were able to get through to him by acting as his advisors. They were able to show how his own behavior might have been sabotaging the results he wanted based upon the choices he made. As Mike demonstrated more acceptance of the process, he began to take more responsibility for his actions. His parents empowered Mike with choices and opportunities that encouraged him to take charge of the situation.

In discussing the possibilities of altering his choices for classes until he becomes accustomed to the new school, for example, Mike agreed that making a few changes in his first semester might be in his best interest. Mike also admitted his physical complaints and refusal to go to school was due to feeling overwhelmed and anxious concerning his ability to follow through on assignments.

Fearing he'd fall behind and receive anything less than an A was something he was not willing to face. Developing physical complaints was his logical answer to the problem. Mike and his parents agreed to change his class schedule until he could comfortably take on AP classes, and his physical complaints disappeared.

Providing Mike with alternatives stimulated his ability to take charge and incorporate changes that maintained his control over his environment. This Negotiating approach also gave Mike the emotional control he needed to continue to take charge of his life.

Issues regarding sports and peers were a bit more difficult. Both dealt with Mike being willing to invest more in others. In both of these cases, it was up to Mike to decide whether or not he enjoyed accepting direction from a coach and being a team player.

When he was honest with himself, Mike realized this was something he wasn't willing to do. However, he still was interested in looking for athletic outlets.

Golf became an option. Mike and his father began playing on weekends, and eventually this resulted in him joining the school golf team.

As Mike calmed down and began to experience some positive accomplishments and interactions, he became more willing, with the help of a counselor, to face his difficulties in dealing with his peers. He began to take a closer look at his behavior, and worked on getting along with others better.

Using the Negotiating approach and parenting a kid like Mike requires extra patience from the parents, as well as commitment on the part of the child. At any time through the process, Mike could have closed down and refused to work with his parents. By not dictating or demanding Mike's compliance, but instead stimulating his action through discussion,

Mike's parents were able to get him to take a realistic look at the behavior he was demonstrating.

If Mike had chosen not to respond, his parents could have moved into a Directing mode and taken more control away from Mike. This also may have eventually gotten Mike on track, but with a lot more stress on all involved.

Mike is highly compliant, independent, and a strong initiator—like most kids who respond well to Negotiating mode. They are more self-reliant, involved, and results-oriented. They know what's expected and perform well at home and school. They require little direction and even less support than a participatory child, because they are achievement-driven and have a well-established sense of self-confidence and motivation.

The Negotiating approach worked for Mike. His parents were able to help him significantly by advising him, showing guidance and reinforcement, being involved, and paying attention to his needs.

The previous examples prove that just like these parents, with the right support you can use Parental GPS to figure out what approach to use to help your children when they get off track and elevate their performance to their highest degree of competency. The parents in the examples above incorporated Directing, Coaching, Participating, or Negotiating tactics after reading their kids' world and figuring out what approach might work best. By asserting a leadership position, these parents were able to guide their children out of some very tricky situations and back toward feeling accomplished and motivated.

The leadership these parents incorporated by redirecting their child's behavior resulted in improved performance, but more importantly, instilled the self-esteem, confidence, and motivation their kids needed to become self-sustaining, stable, successful adults.

What's Next?

Congrats! These first three chapters have presented you with a new method for recognizing and understanding what goes on in the lives of your children. You've learned how to effectively pay attention to your kids and apply 21st Century Parenting. Now comes the real work, the constant application of 21st Century Parenting to achieve the results you desire.

At the conclusion of each year, my Outreach Concern counselors compile statistics from the schools we've worked with. This information presents various areas of opportunity regarding parent-child interaction that we'll focus on for the upcoming school year. Over the past five years, we've recognized some constant challenges for parents and children toward the development of healthy families. The following chapters provide parents insight into those challenges.

CHAPTER 4

When Parents Are Roadblocks

*"At the end of the day, the most
overwhelming key to a child's success is
the positive involvement of parents."*
—Jane D. Hull

*Julia, an eighth grader, brings a pack of razor blades to school
and passes them out to her girlfriends. She tells them about*
cutting: *"This helps when you get in trouble with your parents
or just feel bad," she says, and encourages her classmates to
try it. One of them reports this incident to her own parents,
who then notify the school. When Julia's mother is called and
informed of her daughter's behavior, she responds, "I know
Julia cuts. She's been doing this for a while. It's no big deal,
many of the girls her age do it."*

*Mark is a sixth grader, a transplant to California from
the Midwest. He used to be active in sports, very social, and
a strong student. Recently his grades have fallen. He refuses
to engage in sports and has difficulty making friends. He's
been telling his parents he doesn't like the new school. He
comes home one afternoon with a cut under his eye and says
he doesn't know how he got it. He continues to tell his parents*

about his dissatisfaction, begging them to take him out of the school. The following week he's found with a bottle of prescription medication and is threatening to jump off the school's third-floor balcony. The school counselor discovers Mark's been bullied since the beginning of the new year, and recently the taunting got physical to the point where he is now frightened to go to classes.

Jimmy is fifteen years of age when he shows up at school intoxicated. He passes out and is immediately sent to the hospital, where his stomach is pumped. He's suspended from school for five days. His mother argues with the principal and refuses to talk to the counselors who offer support services for her son. This is the fourth school Jimmy has attended in two years. When the principal attempts to address Jimmy's behavior, his mother begins to insist his teacher is causing him a great deal of stress and classmates have bullied him. The following weekend Jimmy is arrested at a local movie theater for being intoxicated and passing out in front of the theater.

Getting Help

Each year our counselors, like other professionals throughout the country, are referred thousands of kids similar to these examples. The reasons relate to various academic, behavioral, social, emotional, health, and family issues. Some problems can be resolved with a helpful ear and a bit of direction—grades improve, organization increases, homework is turned in, or a child learns how to develop more friends. Some need more help.

All too often there are issues of greater concern: Learning disabilities, ADHD, absenteeism, depression, divorce, custody issues, remarriage, child abuse—it's a long list, and each issue alone increases the emotional temperatures for children and others responsible for their welfare.

Unfortunately, children plagued with these problems bring far more to the classroom, home, and society than their books and pencils. Confronted with these problems on a daily basis, their ability to cope and to demonstrate success in various aspects of their lives is often seriously impacted.

In some cases, the help they need can be provided by in-school services, counselors, and/or the school psychologist. However, many of these situations necessitate support from outside sources such as counseling, testing, tutoring, or medication. Until this intervention is incorporated into a child's life, his behavior often worsens and his success and sometimes health and welfare continue to be seriously impacted. Unfortunately, a major contributor to the problem often turns out to be the parents, who are sometimes more of a "Roadblock" to their child's success rather than a supporter.

Through our work in schools we have found that even after parents were contacted and provided information on the difficulties their children were experiencing, upwards of 60 percent didn't respond to suggestions or referrals; of those parents who did, less than 50 percent followed through. For those who don't respond, their child continues to flounder, and the child's problems intensify; the child joins the ever-growing population of "at-risk" children.

What's it like for an at-risk child? Each day the child walks into the classroom with less at her disposal to be a successful student and she doesn't know why. After a while, some don't care. They may show up and look like and act like other students, but when it comes to performance, they stumble. They can't stay on-task, don't respond to directions, are unorganized, can't process information, don't turn in assignments, don't complete schoolwork—the list goes on.

Physical, psychological, and educational challenges cause these children to fall further behind the kids they sit next to each day. While many of their peers are progressing, they see Ds and Fs and hear about their nonperformance from teachers, administrators, and sometimes parents, all of which further impacts their emotional temperature, self-esteem, self-concept, and motivation.

They hear about their poor performance and don't have the tools or skills to incorporate a change. Their nonresponsive parent supports their failure via lack of attention. Continued failure places the child behind his or her classmates, sometimes stimulating emotional temperatures that develop out of control. These failures create a negative picture of school, the classroom, teachers, and the entire learning process, resulting in children who want nothing to do with school because it's a place they feel *pain*.

Continued failures impact their esteem, confidence, and motivation. Their emotional temperatures run high due to conflicts with teachers and parents regarding their performance, resulting in a downward spiral emotionally, behaviorally, and academically, often demonstrating inappropriate self-destructive behavior. Sometimes they turn to more aggressive at-risk behavior—dropping out of school or making inappropriate choices that may negatively impact them the rest of their lives, like Mike.

> *I would walk into a classroom and immediately hate where I was. I didn't fit in, didn't feel good, and immediately disliked the teacher and sometimes the other kids. I can't remember ever feeling good about school other than meeting a few friends and getting high. I would count the minutes until recess or lunch, hoping I could get there without the teacher calling on me with a question I couldn't answer that would make me feel stupid and embarrassed. I watched other kids getting tests back year after year with As, Bs, and Cs and I was happy if I got by with a D. In most cases, I did worse.*
>
> *I can't remember when school wasn't a boring waste of time. Occasionally, I would have a teacher who seemed cool, but most just seemed to go through the motions, reminding me how I was stupid or didn't try or needed to try or didn't care, and sometimes they were right. It was the same thing*

day after day. I heard, "Pay attention" from teachers, and "Where's your homework?" My parents harassed me about my grades, missing assignments, being late, the calls they got from teachers, but usually they didn't do much more than that—thank God, I thought.

Even when I tried, which wasn't often, I couldn't get it. Occasionally, my parents spent time with me on homework, but it always felt like hours dragging by and it always ended up in a battle.

At times I'd actually go to school and feel I could pass a test I really studied for. Then I wouldn't remember the answers and, of course, failed. Each day was miserable; school seemed a punishment. So I started coming late, missing classes, ditching, lying about my homework, and hiding my grades from my parents.

When I was in the fourth grade my parents took me to a doctor and put me on some kind of medication. I didn't like how I felt when I was taking it. I fought with my parents for three weeks until they let me stop.

Then, in sixth grade, things got better. I met a guy and we started smoking pot after school. I'd get high every day, sometimes before I went to school. When I went to high school we'd leave at lunch and go get stoned. It's how I spent my day, getting high and staying high so I didn't have to hear what I wasn't doing or should've been doing. Detentions mounted up, and I got suspended. My parents were always dragging me back to school, they'd complain about all that I wasn't doing, and I'd make promises I knew I wouldn't keep. Finally, in my junior year, I just quit it and dropped out.

I finally escaped from "school hell," but I had no idea what hell I was walking into. I never graduated, got busted, was on and off probation, had no car, no skills, just friends

who did what I did: got high every day. I had a few jobs, but
usually I lost them because I either didn't show up or went to
work high and got fired.

Mike finally landed a good job in his thirties—one of the most dangerous jobs in the world: he became a deep-sea diver. His life started to change; he bought a condo and attempted to go back to school. Unfortunately, throughout this time he continued to abuse alcohol and other drugs, and more than once lost good opportunities. Mike entered a number of treatment programs, but never followed through. Finally, Mike was found intoxicated on the job and let go; two weeks later he was found in a hotel room dead from a drug overdose.

No, not every child who has challenges ends their life like Mike; however, in many cases, their prospects aren't bright because of a history of failure; Mike's problems began with his parents not paying attention, which followed him throughout his life. Unfortunately, his parents blamed the school, teachers, and counselors, making excuses for his behavior when they should have been redirecting it. In some cases, they identified their own lives as being overwhelmed with issues, which in their estimation made it impossible to follow through on Mike's issues. In general, they simply resisted being parents, and Mike paid the price.

Parental resistance is sadly commonplace. Not responding to a child's needs in a timely manner can aggravate a bad situation, heightening a child's emotional temperature as he moves further from expected results and the positive feelings that accompany them to negative emotions and behaviors that further sabotages his success. As his issues accelerate and his needs grow greater neither the problem nor the world the child lives in stands still. As expectations continue to increase, the child's ability to maintain and perform successfully lessens, further impacting how he feels about himself and his ability to change his behavior.

The goal and responsibility of parents is to read their children's environment, recognize what's going on in their world, and meet the needs of their children, providing them the best opportunity and support to meet life's challenges. This means responding to whatever special needs are identified, moving away from a defensive, indecisive posture that anchors children to nonperformance, negatively impacting how they view themselves.

The antidote for the child is a parent's response. If contacted by someone from your child's school offering support regarding your child's needs, listen. Recognize there's no stigma associated with a child who's challenged or in need of professional help, except if the parent attaches one to it. The major goal of the healthcare experts in and outside of your child's school is to partner with you, providing your child the assistance he or she needs to drive his or her success.

Take action and investigate the options. Remember, though, that the longer you allow your child to fail due to an unresolved issue you're not responding to, the more heightened the negative impact on your child's present and future performance, health, and welfare.

If your child runs out in front of a car, what do you do? Of course, you protect him. If during play she falls off a swing and breaks her arm, do you let it heal itself? Of course not, you take her to your doctor to have it set. If your child comes down with the flu, you take him to his pediatrician. In each of these cases you respond, and quickly. Why not respond to a teacher or counselor with the same sense of urgency? The concerns identified are just as problematic, and they involve your child's health and welfare. Most physical injuries are remedied with quick medical intervention; not responding to these issues risks giving the child a lifelong physical problem. It is the same with a learning, behavioral, or emotional issue; not responding with the sense of urgency you give to physical injuries may cause a child long-term and possibly lifetime problems—ones that may be difficult to reverse.

What's in the best interest of your children? It's your job to find out. What are you willing to do in order for them to compete, perform, and progress? To guide them toward leading a life of positive change?

Professional intervention gives your children the step up they need versus a life sentence of nonperformance.

If your children can't function in a classroom or in life—due to challenges they didn't ask for and don't know how to remedy—then they need help. In most cases they don't even understand what success looks like because they haven't experienced it. They do, however, know what it feels like to fail because that's their living experience. The only person who can remedy this is you. Recognize that every day you don't take action is another day they fall further behind both in performance and emotional well-being.

So what does intervention look like? It may be counseling, testing, school accommodations, tutoring, parental support, parenting classes, and in some cases, medication. But before you say no, get involved; get informed.

In most cases you're going to get a call from your child's teacher, principal, or school counselor. They are going to tell you something you probably don't want to hear: "There's something wrong." Your child is under-performing, can't stay on tasks, doesn't respond to direction, doesn't complete homework, or doesn't interact well with other students. This isn't a life sentence.

Yes, it's a call nobody wants to receive, but recognize they're not saying your child is a bad student or you're a bad parent. They're not saying your child can't be successful; it's that he or she is not *being* successful and there's a possible remedy. Move away from your defensive posture; ask questions, be involved, and be willing to accept their suggestions; question what you don't understand, and develop a dialogue and partnership with everyone who is educating your child.

Remember, you and your child need help to remedy this problem. Go back to the broken arm example: you wouldn't attempt to set your child's arm yourself; you'd let a doctor do the job because they are an expert and they're operating in the best interest of your child's health. This issue relates to your child's lifelong health; it's the same thing, and it answers the question of what's in the best interest of your child's health and welfare and future success.

Do your research. Ask professionals, become knowledgeable about what's available, and find the alternative that provides the relief and direction your child needs. Establishing a meaningful and rewarding experience for your children today will bring benefits to their future. Take responsibility for your children's success, examine every option, but be open and fair to your children, too—their success depends upon your responsiveness.

CHAPTER 5

Parental Leadership: What It Is and How to Use It

"A leader is one who knows the way,
goes the way, and shows the way."
—John C. Maxwell

I'm watching a young family with a five-year-old having breakfast. Like many kids he's bored; he had a few bites of food, and now wants to investigate something more interesting than listening to his mom and dad's conversation. He begins to stand up on his chair. His mother chimes in with "Bobby, Mommy doesn't like it when you stand on chairs." Bobby is totally disinterested in Mom's feeble attempt to get her message across and continues climbing. Mom responds, "Bobby, if you don't get down you could hurt yourself." Again, no response from Bobby, and soon the chair's beginning to tip and, of course, eventually it falls. Bobby lets out a yell as does Mom when he hits the floor. The she says, "See Bobby, you didn't listen to Mom and you fell."

Dad has not been paying much attention, but now he jumps in with "Bobby, why don't you listen to your mother when she asks you to do something?" Bobby, crying, looks

dazed at his parents. Finally he gets back in the chair. Now
Mom and Dad begin discussing with Bobby why he should
listen, asking if he doesn't understand that when Mommy
and Daddy say no, they mean no, etc., etc.

This is parenting, but a bad example. Once again, parents aren't paying attention. It's a common example in which parents negotiate, bargain, beg, and plead as they attempt to get their children to "psychologically buy into the right thing to do" instead of just telling Bobby what he needs to do. What's missing: *leadership.*

Parental leadership tells everyone in the family that someone's in charge, but more importantly it establishes structure and security for those involved. That means sometimes a parent needs to make an "unpopular decision" because it's the right thing to do versus demonstrating an indifferent, permissive, or entitled approach, which often leads to problems and emotional temperatures that collide between parents and children due to the lack of leadership.

Jake is twelve years old, athletic, and his family lives at the
beach, so they enjoy water sports, fishing, boating, surfing.
When Jake's father was his age and living in the same area,
he was pretty independent, allowed to go to the beach with his
friends and surf with little parental supervision. Jake now
wants that same privilege and often argues with his parents
as to why they don't "trust him" enough to allow him to go
independent of their supervision. As heated discussions often
arise, Jake's parents stand their ground and won't allow him
to go without them.

Jake's parents are making a tough unpopular decision regarding Jake's request, incorporating a strong parental leadership position, recognizing that things were different thirty-five years ago and that they aren't willing to make their son's safety and welfare a negotiable issue. Obviously, this is not a popular decision with Jake, who doesn't understand his parents' position regarding how today's environment has changed and presents obstacles and challenges now that were not present when Jake's father was his age.

What is parental leadership? It is maintaining structure, security, safety, and support for a child through setting boundaries. Boundaries set limits on a child's behavior; they also reward children for their attention to parental expectations. Boundaries establish structure, guidelines, and reinforcement for desired behavior while helping to eliminate poor, nonresponsive behavior. The lack of parental boundary-setting is the number one complaint identified by counselors over a twenty-five-year period in my school-based counseling program, Outreach Concern.

Boundaries establish guidelines and safety for children, providing them with the sense of security they need. Even more importantly, boundaries introduce them to the fact that someone will always be establishing ground rules, guidelines, and direction for their behavior throughout their lives.

Children learn self-management through boundary settings; those who learn to respond to boundaries early in life have it easier in life. They walk into a classroom knowing how to respond to teachers and other students. They know how to perform on the playground, how to navigate through elementary, middle, high school, and on to college; they recognize how to effectively conduct themselves throughout life. Those who embrace the importance of rules learn to self-manage and discipline themselves toward successful outcomes.

Establishing boundaries for your children early in life establishes a pattern for their success in all areas, making life easier for them to *participate in* rather than just survive. Boundaries provide them with appreciation and support for their efforts and successes, as well as help them to view their shortcomings as learning opportunities. Knowing where boundaries lie and how to successfully maneuver through them toward successful outcomes helps a child establish a healthy sense of self,

one that looks forward to new opportunities and welcomes challenges
and is more likely to experience success.

So, Mom and Dad, become comfortable with establishing boundaries.
Realize that being a strong, effective parent is sometimes about being
willing to make decisions that are not popular with your children, but
that are made in the best interest of your children, leading to their
lifelong success.

> Each month Connie, fifteen, and her mother go to the mall to
> "window shop." Mom sees this as an opportunity for her and
> her daughter to bond and spend some special time together.
> Her daughter's favorite shop is Forever 21. After looking at
> the outfits in the window, Connie persuades her mother to
> enter the store. Mom reminds Connie, "Remember we're just
> window shopping, we're not buying anything today." Connie
> looks through the stacks of tops, grabs a blouse, a sweater,
> and a pair of jeans, leaving her mom behind as she enters
> the fitting room. Connie comes back out and peers into the
> mirror, admiring how she looks. Her mother reminds her
> again, "Connie remember, we're not buying anything today;
> just looking." Connie retreats to the fitting room, reappearing
> with the articles she tried on and presents them to the sales
> associate at the cash register. Mom again reminds Connie that
> they didn't come to buy. Connie retorts, "Mom, don't make a
> scene, get over it." All of which results in Mom purchasing
> Connie's new clothes. Month after month the same scenario
> presents itself, with Mom and Connie entering the store to
> "just look," and Connie walking out with new clothes her
> mother wasn't ready to buy, but does so to avoid an argument.
>
> One Friday rolls around and this time Dad decides
> to accompany his wife and daughter on their monthly
> expedition. After lunch the three go through the mall, when
> once again Connie enters her favorite store and again hears

her mother's familiar statement, "We're looking and not buying today." Connie again grabs a handful of clothes, tries them on, and presents them to the sales associate, and once more Mom objects. Connie abruptly retorts in a similar fashion, "Mom get over it, just give her your credit card." But before Mom takes out her wallet, Dad grabs his wife and escorts her out of the store, leaving Connie, the clothes, and the sales associate without a credit card. Embarrassed, Connie leaves the store without her new clothes. Since that time, when Connie and her mom go shopping, she no longer pulls the same stunt.

Being a parent isn't about friendship. It's about leadership. It's about taking charge responsibly and asserting your expectations, establishing boundaries. Leadership doesn't suggest compliance; it demands it. Today, too many parents are more interested in being their child's friend versus getting their child to perform.

Friendship is based on appreciation for an individual, respect, consideration, and responsibility; and it's mutual. In the example, Connie wasn't interested in a relationship with her mother; she wasn't considerate of her mother's wishes or respectful of her mother's directives. She was interested in Connie and what she wanted and was willing to get it at any cost.

So if you want a friend, get a dog. They're often more responsive, loyal, and will appreciate you more than your children might at various times in their lives. Stop asking your children to be something they don't know how to be and in many cases are unwilling to be—certainly not with their parents.

Be a parent who leads first and becomes a friend later—try ten or twenty years later, when your adult child understands what parent-child relationships are all about. Until then, you're going to call the shots and make the decisions. Your job is to develop your child into a responsible, independent adult. That's what's in it for you and eventually for him or her, and this requires your leadership.

What's Wrong with No?

As previously stated, sometimes parental leadership is about making the *tough unpopular decision*. It's about saying *no* even when *yes* would be more popular, easier, and wouldn't create waves. But as a parent, sometimes you're going to create waves today in order to minimize storms tomorrow.

What is it about the word *No* that keeps parents from using it? *No* is one of the clearest, most direct statements a parent can make. Equally strong is its opposite, *Yes*. The key is to not mistake one for the other. If you're more concerned about popularity than compliance and performance, then don't complain about the results—the behavior your children demonstrate when they've been hearing *Yes* when they should have heard *No*.

What is *no* all about? It's about safety, structure, time, cost, performance, and discipline. *No* exists for a reason. If you have a reason and *no* is the proper response, then say, "No!" Saying no to your children prepares them for the many nos they're going to receive in life.

No doesn't mean anything but no! There's nothing attached like "I don't like you" and "You're a bad kid." *No* stands on its own. And no, you don't always need to provide your child with a reason. In fact, don't get in the habit of providing one as it creates a precedent that says well if you didn't like *no*, then let's discuss it. That suggests your *no* is soft, that your child doesn't have to believe it, and that your *no* is open to negotiation. Besides, hearing *no* can be a great motivator; it can make your child work harder, be more responsible next time, and give you a reason to say yes somewhere down the line.

Is Anyone Listening? Maybe Not!

You know what's great about TV, radio, and the internet? You can turn them off when you've had enough, particularly when those annoying commercials or pop-ups interrupt you. You're watching something and every fifteen minutes or so the volume on the TV goes up and someone starts selling you something you have no interest in, so you hit the mute button.

Unfortunately, some parents sound similar to those commercials. In attempting to address an issue or concern with their children, they come across as an advertisement, commercializing their request, which results in their disinterested listener switching the parent off.

Some parents have great relationships with their children and communicate openly, achieving the response they desire; whereas others, with the same goals, fall short of achieving their desired response. They don't recognize it's often due to the behavior they demonstrate when attempting to converse with their child that negatively impacts their child's willingness to both listen and respond appropriately. The result: the child hits the parent mute button.

Zinging

Is it because parents are boring? Maybe, but actually it's because sometimes they overdo it. It's about *zinging*—those annoying patterns of communication some parents incorporate as a vehicle to drive their message. In fact, zinging actually has more to do with a child's lack of responsiveness than the parent's request; it often accelerates a child's emotional temperature instead of getting them to engage with parents and achieving the desired outcome parents expect.

Zinging is the Maximizing, Minimizing, Catastrophe-zing, Generalizing, Horrible-zing, Commercializing, Hysterical-zing, Historical-zing, Moralizing, and Sermonizing parents wrap their message around in a feeble attempt to make a point. Unfortunately, this behavior causes a child to spend more time looking for the parent turnoff switch than attentively listening to the parent's message. Additionally, this response often incites so much emotionality in the child that the actual point of the message is lost, with the listener becoming defensive and non-participative.

Zinging examples have a number of problems in common, all of which seriously impact communication. First, they water down the real message—the point the parent is attempting to make. They separate and create more distance between you and your child, because the message affixes a negative critique and emotion toward the child and their behavior. Additionally, they suggest the child is not capable or competent enough to change the behavior. When used consistently, they give the child the idea that any time the parent approaches him or her with a direction, he or she is going to hear more of the same; so if your goal is to make your child feel bad, not pay attention, or be remorseful and generally turn you off, by all means, continue incorporating zinging into your conversations. However, if you want to develop healthy communication channels, mutual problem-solving, and a real partnership that will get your child to buy in and work with you, stop zinging.

How to Get Your Message Heard

As seen in the zinging example, children and adolescents will do anything to keep from experiencing negative emotions, and if that means turning the parent off to keep that from happening, that's exactly what they are going to do. So now that you've stopped zinging, try to be specific with your goal: what is it you want to change? "I want my child to do his homework"; "I want her to get home on time"; "I want him to pick up his room." First, establish your goal; now, let's work on your delivery.

Your message is important and you want your child to provide an expected result, so you need to get your listener's attention. When's the best time to address an issue? Just like anything you're attempting to sell, parental timing is everything. The worst time to focus on addressing an issue is in the middle of an argument or when you or your child is emotionally impacted by some other problem or concern. Approaching her with another issue is going to escalate her emotional temperature and cause her to close down or defend her position rather than be open to hearing you. Remember, your goal is to effect some type of change. You want to approach your child when her emotional temperature welcomes and accepts a conversation.

Because kids often have a tendency to be on the defensive side when their parents approach them, begin your conversation with something positive that they've done. "Hey Rick, I noticed you brought up your test scores in math, great job." "Bob, thanks for putting some gas in the car last night, I didn't have time to do it this morning and you saved me some time." Now address what you need them to do. The concept of incorporating something positive takes them off their defensive position and opens them up to being more receptive to what might come next.

Now incorporate your request, direction, or expectation. Be specific, short, and to the point; don't attack, generalize, or pile on issues as these can overwhelm a child. Request the change you want to see. Ask for feedback or clarification. Establish the groundwork that will solicit and support their response and try to keep the conversation from being one-dimensional or one-sided. Remember what you are striving for is their participation in the process. Talk about *present* changes; don't tie it to the future. Make sure you get a commitment regarding the change you're asking for. Thank them, and end the conversation.

Now move away from your issue. Address something else. Don't tie your request to anything, and don't pile on other issues or requests. Stay out of lecture mode and away from anything that attacks them on a personal level.

Remember that children, particularly adolescents, have a tendency to take things personally and may use some of the zinging themselves, like generalizing: "Gee Mom, you're always on my case; Dad, you never give me the time I need to complete something." Sidestep their response. Don't respond to their generalization; respond with a clear statement about what you're asking. Keep in mind that the idea isn't to make them lose, but for both of you to win, because you need their partnership.

It's about talking *with*, not *at* your child and establishing complementary interaction. Establishing mutually rewarding parent-child interaction by being clear, specific, and participative will provide you the relationship you want with your child today, but it will also establish healthy communication channels that allow him or her to demonstrate the rest of his or her life, benefiting his or her present and future endeavors.

Acknowledge Attempts, but Only Reward Accomplishments

Recently I was at a Little League award banquet where every player on the team received a trophy. Every kid. The first-place winners as well as the ones who finished last; the ones who participated and tried their hardest, and those who missed practices and didn't show up for games—each child received a trophy. When I inquired as to why everyone received awards, I was told the league believes that every child needs to be recognized and that their parents didn't want any child on a team not to be acknowledged.

Really? The children who didn't win or who didn't show up for practice or games didn't participate—they should be rewarded because at times they wore a uniform and not giving them a trophy was going to somehow destroy them? The message here is that a child's self-esteem is so fragile they will be crushed when they don't get an award for doing nothing.

In any race there's only one winner: the person who crosses the finish line first. The rest are race participants. They did well, worked toward their goal, but they did not win. In hockey there is only one winner of the Stanley Cup. The Super Bowl awards only one Lombardi trophy. In golf, the Green Jacket of the Masters goes to the winner only. In life, like in sports, there are varying degrees of success. There are people and teams who finish in first place, and then there is all the rest. We, of course, applaud all the players, we affirm their efforts, but we only celebrate the ones who finish in first place.

Once the child reaches adult life, no one is going to provide him with a trophy for nonparticipation, for not achieving her sales goal, his quota, not completing a report that was due on Friday until late the following Wednesday. No one will say, "Great job, here is a 20 percent pay increase because you were $25,000 under your sales goal."

Participation—and, sometimes, losing—is part of life's process. It builds character and integrity, motivation, and work ethic. Treating everyone who shows up the same way, rewarding all the participants as if they won, waters down the importance of winning, as well as trying. If you believe the opposite, just look at where all those second, third, and participation trophies your kids get end up.

So how should you celebrate and recognize your child's efforts, tasks, and goals? In short: *Acknowledge Attempts, But Only Reward and Celebrate Accomplishments.* As a parent you want your child to be motivated, and showing up and participating is only half of the game. No one applauds missing a three-point shot or not catching a pass or not getting on base, and they shouldn't; however, they applaud the effort. Not establishing a difference between effort and accomplishment minimizes and weakens self-esteem, self-concept, and motivation.

Be clear and specific in terms of your direction and support. Let your children know you appreciate their attempts and participation, their willingness and ability, but maybe that ability and commitment needs to improve. This makes them recognize your role and interest in their lives. Let them know you believe in their ability to do better, and be willing to provide supportive direction when appropriate. Celebrating their participation as an event, one to be awarded with a monument, sends them a message that just showing up is as important as those who did their best; it's not.

Remember, you always want to be supportive and demonstrate pride in the fact your children are making attempts. However, make a clear differentiation between recognizing they showed up and tried and celebrating how they finish. This provides children an expectation for being great, but more importantly, a view of how they will be judged and acknowledged throughout their life for all their endeavors. Don't celebrate what you don't see; no one else in their life will.

The Ten Commandments of Common Courtesy

It's Saturday afternoon at the local grocery store. The aisles are filled with shoppers, many with baskets full of groceries and children in tow. Some have these little folks in their baskets, some are holding their hands, and others, oblivious to anyone else in the market, are allowing their children to run through the aisles, frustrating shoppers. There is a loud screech and what looks like a six-year-old boy with a pacifier in his mouth running up and down the aisles, bouncing off shoppers and carts as if running through a minefield. As people move out of the way, the boy—who seems to believe the market is his personal playground—continues his attack through the aisles, bumping into people and responding with nothing more than a surprised look at them, as if wondering why they're in his way. Then the boy stops in front of a shopper, plants his feet firmly on the ground, and refuses to move. "Excuse me, buddy, can you let me get by?" the shopper asks. The boy refuses. He grabs the front of the basket and starts pushing. His parents are far behind and do nothing to remedy the problem. Eventually, he takes off; now his two sisters are joining in a chorus of "We can do whatever we want to do, just watch us." Through this entire episode the parents do nothing but continue to shop and occasionally call out to their children.

Today everyone seems to talk about political correctness, but they forget it begins at home with something more important: simple common courtesy and manners. However, as some bright person once said, the one thing uncommon about common courtesy is that it's not common. Why and where does it begin? Well, it's supposed to begin at home, with parents teaching their children basic awareness and consideration of their behavior and how it impacts others. In short, being polite.

Remember these magic words from growing up: *Please* and *Thank you*. I don't know if they're magic, but they sure help you get what you want no matter what age you are, and they still work.

I remember a principal requesting we have our counselors do a workshop on courtesy at her school. When I asked what the problem was, she responded, "Please just show my students how to conduct themselves in public; just basic manners, 'please' and 'thank you!' These kids don't know how to eat, they don't know what a napkin's for, they don't pick up after themselves—it's as if they all took the same class in a 'lack of manners.'"

As a result, we came up with "The Ten Commandments of Common Courtesy." These suggestions apply to all children and adults, providing them the opportunity to present themselves appropriately in all arenas in which they operate. When demonstrated consistently, a kinder, considerate, and more aware child appears, setting him- or herself up for success in the world. All by focusing on the correctness that begins with common courtesy.

The Ten Commandments of Common Courtesy

I. *Thou shalt say "please" and "thank you."* These magic words still have magic.

II. *Thou shalt address adults as "Sir" or "Ma'am," "Miss" or "Mister," and not "Hey you" or by their first name.* It is not being formal; it's showing respect.

III. *Thou shalt shake hands and not bump fists or "high five."* Your child didn't just score a three-point shot.

IV. *Thou shalt not interrupt.* Is everything your child's saying really that important?

V. *Thou shalt say, "Excuse me."* If you must interrupt or get someone's attention.

VI. *Thou shalt close thy mouth when eating.* No, the people around you don't need to be reminded what you're having for lunch.

VII. *Thou shalt learn how to hold a knife, a fork, and what to do with a napkin.* They're utensils not weapons.

VIII. *Thou shalt take off thy hat when entering a room, particularly a restaurant.* Okay, it's a fashion statement, I get it, but a bad one.

IX. This one is for Mom and Dad: *Thou shalt control thy children in public.* Not everyone is as enthusiastic about your children as you are, and not everyone believes all their actions are as cute and sweet as you do.

X. I know I said the "Ten Commandments of Common Courtesy," but there're only nine. The tenth is a fill-in. Take a look at your child from the point of view of another; be objective in regarding what he or she does that may need attention. Now fill in number ten _____ and stick to it.

The key is making common courtesy more common and it begins at home. When parents model and expect this behavior, they are recognizing, requiring their children to pay attention to common courtesy. It isn't really asking anything more than standard operating procedure for appropriate behavior as is expected throughout their life. This investment you make in your children's behavior will not only return personal dividends today, but also provide your children ongoing dividends throughout their lives as they learn how to act appropriately in public, support a set of expected social norms, and receive the respect they might want throughout their lives.

CHAPTER 6

When Your Child Is in School, You're in School, Too

"I cried every day of first grade. In class. Which meant I ended up getting comfortable emoting in a place where it wasn't the norm."
—Jesse Eisenberg

Ask any parent what arguments they have with their children and the subject of school is bound to come up. Issues regarding homework, grades, teachers, follow-through, and performance come to a point, resulting in emotional temperatures running high for all involved. However, school battles don't need to take place if parents focus on the four main areas these arguments surround:

1. Getting started
2. Partnerships
3. Organization
4. Homework

Getting Started: Readiness Training

First, get your children started off the right way and you guarantee fewer arguments and more successful outcomes. Realize if your child is in first grade, so are you. If they're in high school, you're right along with them. If they have a special need, so do you. Every issue, opportunity, problem, or concern is not your child's responsibility, but the partnership you need to establish with him or her and with all other significant position-holders involved in your child's success throughout his or her educational careers.

> *Matt, a six-year-old kindergartner, cries every morning when his mother takes him to school and hides under his desk until she picks him up. Ben, a first-grader, won't sit in his seat and shouts out at the teacher. Jimmy bites other students and runs out of the classroom and hides from his teacher and other students. What's going on?*

Most concerns brought to the attention of teachers and counselors from kindergarten through second grade relate to kids being shocked by school. Why? Because their parents haven't assisted them in making an easy transition from being protected and cared for at home to a new environment that challenges them each day; one that is far less reinforcing than their family environment. Sometimes this results in school being a negative and not a positive experience, heightening a child's emotional temperature and response, and he or she doesn't yet have the skills to effectively deal with this new experience.

Often such acting out with various inappropriate or aggressive responses could have been eliminated if parents would begin working with their children early to "talk up school," that is, getting them ready and socialized to this new experience they'll be participating in for the next twelve years and hopefully more.

Readiness training is making sure children have the ability to enter school with skills, tools, and a positive attitude, ready to be successful. Moreover, readiness training prepares children for school by promoting their physical well-being, their social and emotional development, how they approach learning, language development, and incorporating general knowledge before they enter the classroom.

Readiness training makes children look forward to the first day of school rather than fear it. It arms your child with the ability to walk into a classroom, listen, and respond appropriately, making him ready to be a successful student throughout his educational career. Readiness training helps transition a child from home to school, creating a bridge between early care from parents to teacher-parent partnerships that provide support throughout childhood and adolescence.

Most of all, readiness training is the early and necessary parental commitment to the ongoing success of their children's educational career. Incorporating support and direction that supplements their ongoing success from the first day they enter the classroom should be their parent's number one priority. Overall, readiness training provides a child a helping hand in making her entrance into the educational system a positive, rewarding experience that sets her up for success throughout her educational careers. In school, readiness training, like home training, is the foundation for emotional regulation and acceptance of new opportunities that leads to your child's ongoing educational success.

Ready, Set, Go

The US Department of Education's Office of Communications and Outreach publishes an excellent guide to readiness training entitled "Helping Your Preschool Child." This document introduces various activities and goals for children and parents to incorporate from infancy through age five and it's an excellent vehicle to help prepare a child for school. The items listed below are offered as objectives that children work toward, ones that should become ongoing activities that parents support, directing and encouraging their children to achieve. The checklist focuses on three major areas: Good Health and Physical Well-Being, Social and Emotional Preparation, and Language and General Knowledge. The ongoing incorporation of these goals prepares children to have a positive attitude toward entering school and teaches them to embrace the educational process that will lead them toward successful performance.

Good Health and Physical Well-Being
My child:

- ☐ Eats a balanced diet.
- ☐ Gets plenty of rest.
- ☐ Receives regular medical and dental care.
- ☐ Has had all the necessary immunizations.
- ☐ Runs, jumps, plays outdoors, and does other activities that help develop his large muscles and provide exercise.
- ☐ Works puzzles, scribbles, colors, paints, and does other activities that help develop her small muscles.

Social and Emotional Preparation
My child:

- ☐ Is learning to explore and try new things.
- ☐ Is learning to work well alone and to do many tasks for himself.
- ☐ Has many opportunities to be with other children and is learning to cooperate with them.
- ☐ Is curious and is motivated to learn.
- ☐ Is learning to finish tasks.
- ☐ Is learning to use self-control.
- ☐ Can follow simple instructions.
- ☐ Helps with family chores.

Language and General Knowledge
My child:

- ☐ Has many opportunities to talk and listen.
- ☐ Is read to every day.

☐ Has access to books and other reading materials.

☐ Is learning about print and books.

☐ Has her television and technology viewing monitored by an adult.

☐ Is encouraged to ask questions.

☐ Is encouraged to solve problems.

☐ Has opportunities to notice similarities and differences.

☐ Is encouraged to sort and classify things.

☐ Is learning to write her name and address.

☐ Is learning to count and plays counting games.

☐ Is learning to identify and name shapes and colors.

☐ Has opportunities to draw, listen, make music, and dance.

☐ Has opportunities to get first-hand experiences of doing things in the world—to see and touch objects, hear new sounds, smell and taste foods, and watch things move.

In addition to the readiness suggestions above, the past twenty-five years of working with children from preschool through kindergarten and early elementary school years uncovered additional suggestions to help parents support their children in being successful from the minute they step onto a school campus. Remember the goal is to get your child effectively launched into the educational system, viewing it as a positive experience, one he or she looks forward to versus seeing it as a threat.

This begins with not making school a surprise. We found that thousands of children in preschool or kindergarten are often threatened by school, primarily because it arrives as a surprise to them. This is due to parents not introducing school to their children before they enter the classroom. School needs to be "talked up"; it needs to be part of the family conversation early on in a child's life so that he or she sees school as a rewarding, supportive environment and a natural transition from home. When children have a difficult time separating from parents as they walk into the classroom for the first time, these parents haven't done an effective job in presenting school as a positive experience or opportunity. They haven't equipped their children with the tools to compete.

Part of talking up school begins by making the entire experience less foreign to the child. A child who hasn't been socialized to a classroom, teachers, and other children may respond considerably different and possibly feel threatened by this new experience ho or she doesn't understand. Talking up school is explaining what a teacher does, what happens in a classroom, what it's like to be around other children. Doing so often establishes a comfort level with a child who's going into a new world that's considerably different from the one at home.

A great idea for parents prior to children entering school is to drive by the school your child is going to attend beforehand, to get him or her familiar with the surroundings. Show your child the playground; let him or her see other children play; discuss what school's like; explain what a classroom looks like. If possible, visit a classroom.

Parents need to recognize that teaching a child how to enter school presents the same degree of stress they experience when transitioning into a new job. Everything is new, sometimes exciting, but often frightening. So how can you make the transition from home life—where there may be a good deal of acceptance, support, and involvement from parents and siblings—to school life, where there are other adults who provide direction and who have their own expectations, rules, tasks, and boundaries. In some cases, exposing a child to "school housekeeping" is a way to begin. Providing basic information about what school's all about: school rules, sitting at your desk, raising your hand, not touching other children, not hitting or biting, staying in your seat, following directions. These are the simple everyday behaviors, boundaries, and expectations children will be exposed to and need to demonstrate in order to navigate successfully in the classroom.

Talking up school doesn't end when your child is ready to go to school; it needs to be a continued conversation that parents support on a daily basis. It should incorporate conversations to stimulate thinking about school, supporting your child's efforts and celebrating his or her successes, as well as helping him or her deal with disappointments because school will definitely be a part of your child's life for a minimum of twelve years and hopefully beyond.

Their success—from their daily walk into the classroom until they graduate and beyond—is dependent upon how you establish and support their first step into the classroom. How they enjoy and come to look forward to what will be a large part of their life becomes highly dependent upon how you present and support their entrance and transition, all of which begins with a strong commitment to "Readiness Training."

Partnerships

Those parents who expect a teacher to parent their children when they haven't are always rudely awakened. That first step toward readiness training introduces a child to becoming a successful student, bridging home and school in a comfortable transition. When accomplished, children adjust to school as a new learning and socializing opportunity benefiting all involved.

A big part of that transition is learning how to operate successfully within the educational environment and with new players in a child's life. Therefore, there is also some readiness training needed for parents, regarding the role they must play in their child's educational career. It begins with knowing the role of teacher and parent and the important positions they play in your child's educational experiences. Here's where you set up your child for success or failure in school.

As previously stated, be aware that if your child is in first grade, second grade, or even twelfth grade, so are you. Your child isn't the only one in school—you are, too. If your child has a learning disability, the family has a learning disability. If your child is diagnosed ADHD, so is the family.

This means you have to be aware of the expectations of your child, how he'll be viewed in the classroom, and live it with him. You have to assist the school in making accommodations for the special needs of your child. Be aware of them and make sure you follow through, so that your child gets every break he deserves. But it is up to you to drive this process; it begins by asking yourself what you want school to be. The educational system won't do this for you. It's up to you to be your child's champion, but also to partner with the school in order to achieve the results you need for your child's success.

Look at your child's educational experience like a department store. The school is the store, the teacher is the sales associate, your child and you are the customers, and education is the product. You expect good customer service from the sales associate—the teacher—and you have a right to. You expect the product to be one of value and high quality and you need to make sure it is.

But there are also expectations of you and your child regarding the behavior that needs to be demonstrated in order to get the best service and the most value from the product. Be involved—by teaching and modeling respect, attending all back-to-school meetings, and emailing the teacher at least on a monthly basis to find out the current level of progress and performance your child is demonstrating. Be aware of special projects, tests, everything that pertains to your child's success. This sends a message to the teacher that you support your child, but also that you expect the best level of service possible. By the way, there's no money-back-guarantee with this product in the education store. You only get one chance and you can't bring your child back for an educational trade-in. So make sure you get it right the first time. Your child's success depends on it and you.

Don't expect the principal, superintendent, or state to hold the teacher accountable. You hold them accountable via your involvement. Forget changing the education system, you're the only "champion" your child needs in school.

Expect your children to perform to the best of their ability, but be involved in the process, beginning with teaching them respect for the school, their teacher, and classmates. Don't expect teachers to be successful in setting boundaries for your child's behavior, if you haven't. They're not the experts with your child, you are.

Stop being so eager to believe your children when they complain about their teacher—their lack of fairness, how they give too much homework, or how everybody got a poor grade on the Spanish test. Ask yourself: what does good performance look like? Be specific, lay out clear expectations for your children's behavior, and follow through by monitoring and managing their performance both at home and in school.

Successful Parent-Teacher Partnerships:

Would you give your life savings to an investment broker you never met? Purchase a home you never saw? Buy a car you never drove? So why put your children's future in the hands of teachers you don't know? Since the investment in your child's future is of the utmost importance, closely managing that investment should be paramount in your thinking. You begin by being involved in your children's education, holding both them and their teachers accountable, which guarantees you get the best return on your educational investment in your children.

As previously stated, developing strong partnerships with your child's teachers becomes an essential part of that investment because it deals with the business of your child's future. When parents view their child's education similar to an investment, they can become more effective in managing their child's progress toward their highest level of achievement to get the best return. This eighteen-year commitment can become a highly significant asset to a child's learning career, which will pay huge dividends now, in your child's future, and for the rest of his or her life.

Parents need to recognize the attention their children need and receive in a classroom is in direct relationship to their involvement with their child's teacher. In order to have those needs realized, parents must support open and ongoing communication channels between themselves and their children's teachers. Leaving your child's academic success solely up to teachers who you have no relationship with may suggest to them you hold a lower classroom expectation for your child and the product the teacher presents. Remember, your child is one of many students in a classroom over twelve years. Whatever goal you have regarding your child's education may not be realized unless you're involved.

From the first day she enters school and on until she graduates, you are handing over your child to someone you don't know. Your child's success, performance, and attitude toward learning are dependent upon teachers who can have a major influence in shaping the way she learns and performs. Don't let this life-shaping experience take place without your involvement. Letting each teacher know you're involved and concerned, that you expect to take an active role in your child's education, puts everyone on notice that you're paying close attention to one of the single most important components of your child's life: her educational success.

Don't wait for quarterly report cards to tell you how well your child is doing before you address an issue that affects your child's performance. Establish your position early and address your expectations regarding your child's education each year.

Begin by taking an active role in parent-teacher meetings. This is an important place to establish a leadership position and develop strong partnerships. Those initial back-to-school meetings can be an opportunity for teachers to identify their classroom expectations, but also one in which parents can walk away with a concept of the teacher's style and classroom expectations. Every opportunity to address your children's teachers further supports the necessary dialogue needed to develop closer relationships with an individual who has a major influence on your child. Approaching this opportunity with questions pertinent to your child's classroom experience helps you be closely involved with his learning experience.

The following is a list of questions parents can pose to teachers regarding the academic, social, emotional, and behavioral development of their child's educational career. These questions also help stimulate discussions on areas where children may need additional attention from parents, teachers, or other experts to help support those who may have educational challenges.

Parent-Teacher Meeting Questions:

- Is my child responding to your direction?
- Does my child work well with others?
- Does my child have a difficult time focusing?
- Is my child's work complete and turned in on time?
- Is my child comfortable and responsive in class?
- Does my child answer when called upon in class? How often do they respond with the appropriate answer?
- Does my child turn in completed homework assignments?
- Does my child stay on task?
- Does my child remain focused when you're presenting material?
- Does my child participate in class?
- Does my child work independently or need excessive direction?
- Does my child follow classroom rules?
- Does my child socialize with other students?
- How's my child's performance in relationship to other students in the class?

As you review these questions, you'll recognize this is going to take time. Great—time is what you have. Remember, we're talking about your child, your investment. Obviously, parent-teacher meetings have time limits, so if you need additional time to address issues that require more attention, request a second meeting.

I believe face-to-face meetings versus emailing back and forth are more beneficial for the initial meeting. It's always important to put a face with a name, and parents who show up to these meetings make a stronger statement about their involvement and commitment. Also, visiting your child's classroom can tell you a lot about a teacher, how organized they are, their expectations of students, and overall presentation.

Once you've established that relationship, then communicating by email or phone may be something you and the teacher agree to incorporate. At that initial meeting, however, you need to be considerate of the teacher's time, so come prepared. Address your expectations from your child's academic, social, emotional, and behavioral standpoint. Discuss areas of need you're aware of regarding your child, as the teacher may not be aware of them, and obviously needs to know in order to provide the best possible learning experience.

Are you satisfied with the information you received? Follow-up with an email expressing your appreciation for the teacher's time, addressing any issues or concerns and when you next plan to address these issues with the teacher. If you're not satisfied, request another meeting. Keep in mind that you may hear about issues or concerns regarding your child that you don't understand or don't agree with, so be open to feedback and ask questions. This way everyone will be on the same page regarding your child. A typical parent letter could look like the following:

Ms. Haines
XYZ Elementary School

Dear Ms. Haines:

Thank you for the opportunity to meet with you last Tuesday at the parent-teacher meeting. Both my husband and I appreciated the time you spent providing us valuable insight as to what this year's going to look like for Mark in third grade.

We appreciated your suggestions and will make a point of reading with Mark for thirty minutes each evening in the effort to enhance his reading and comprehensive skills. Thank you for that suggestion. We look forward to hearing any additional suggestions you can offer.

Feel free to email me any time there is a concern or issue. I look forward to speaking with you throughout the year.

Sincerely,
Mrs. Interested Parent

Once again, be open to the suggestions and recommendations from teachers and counselors. The goal is to establish an informed partnership to support your child's success. With a parent-teacher team that works together, everyone—students, parents, and teachers—succeeds, supporting the ongoing development of your child from the day he or she enters school until graduation and beyond.

If this all sounds a bit businesslike, it is. It's part of the business of raising your children, making sure their educational experience is meaningful, and that your children and you get the best educational return on your investment. Remember, don't expect something from teachers or the educational system they can't or may not be willing to provide— particularly if you're not involved. Take charge and be an active participant in your child's educational career and the results you both will achieve will be well worth your investment.

Organization

Organization follows an individual throughout his or her life. Simply put, the more organized a child is, the more successful he or she will be. His or her work product is going to look better, he or she is going to be on time, and his or her result is going to be appreciated to a higher degree.

In the organization game, parents invest in a variety of new-fangled accessories guaranteed to help organize their child each year. Every school supply store sells organization tools to help you organize your children. Just think of the backpack—what an invention!

Every luggage manufacturer has made a fortune on backpacks that you wear over your arm, on your back, push in front, or drag behind. They have wheels, zippers, compartments; they are made of cloth and canvas and come in every color of the rainbow. However, no matter how large or small the bag, kids don't get it. Look in any six- to seventeen-year-old's backpack, if you dare, and you'll find numerous wadded-up pieces of paper, books, chewing gum, old candy wrappers, and broken pencils. There may even be a small community of something living in the bottom. And, of course, they're filled with a variety of those unused organizational tools parents purchase to help their children improve their organizational skills. However, that's the problem: they have to be used in order to be useful.

Here's a simple tool my counselors utilize in schools that helps get kids organized: Go out and purchase one red manila folder and one green manila folder. The red folder is for anything your child is given in school. Explain that all that's supposed to come home—tests, assignments, work sheets, etc.—goes in the red folder. When your child does come home, the first thing you do is ask to see the red folder. Once all the homework is completed and the red folder is empty, take the completed work that needs to go back to school and put it in the green folder. This leaves the red folder empty and the green folder full of work that needs to be taken to school. No other organizational tools are needed. If this sounds too simple, it's because it needs to be.

This doesn't mean you won't continue to find various other surprises in your child's backpack, but it does provide a simple way of organizing children and greatly increases the chances that you'll see what needs to come from school and go back in an expedient manner.

Homework

Homework: do you know anyone who didn't hate homework when they were in school? When you were a kid, how many friends did you hear say, "Gee, I can't wait to get home from school and start in on my homework?" So stop trying to sell your kids on something they don't want to buy. Let them complain about homework, blow off some steam. Quit fighting their opinion about homework; you're only interested in it being completed.

The number one issue parents and children fight over ten months a year is homework. How many times have you asked your son or daughter, "Did you finish your homework?" or "Did you have homework tonight?" only to hear "I did it in school" or "We didn't have any tonight"—and then received a progress report identifying incomplete assignments, all suggesting that your child is in jeopardy of failing.

With today's technology, many schools have incorporated an online process in which parents can dial up their child's grades and identify where their child is academically. This is if the teacher is keeping it regularly updated. The pat answer most parents hear from their kids when presented negative online information is "Well, Ms. Smith hasn't entered my most recent test scores yet," or "Mr. Brown doesn't update grades until the end of the month." No matter what modern miracle schools come up with to help parents and kids deal with the dreaded issue of grades and homework, kids will find a way to manipulate their way out of it. Okay, that's part of being a kid.

For years, parents have been willing to pay experts extraordinary fees to get them to somehow magically come up with an idea to assist them in getting their kids to do homework. If you incorporate the following, you'll be in control of the process, your children's homework will be complete, their grades will improve, and you'll save a lot of money.

First, you already know your child's attitude toward homework and, let's say to be nice she has a tendency to fabricate the process and her commitment to it. Children who participate and take responsibility for their homework usually are a bit more proactive, as their grades would indicate. However, every once in a while, a parent may hear, "Why should I have to do my homework, I get As on tests anyway." This is sometimes a difficult argument to address, but you have to drive the process anyway. Incorporating the following will put you in charge of the homework issue.

Taking Charge of Homework

- Each year, meet your child's teacher at back-to-school nights and get his or her expectation regarding homework. Write it down to use later.
- Get the teacher's email address and phone number and contact him or her on a monthly basis regarding your child's progress in class as well as homework.
- If the school has an online system, learn about it and speak to each teacher and identify how often he or she updates it. Also, get the school's policies regarding this process to make sure the teacher is in compliance.
- Once you have all the data from the teacher and the school, sit down with your child and go over what you now know. This way you and your children know what each teacher expects and what you're going to do to reinforce it.
- Each time you connect with your child's teacher or counselor, make sure you go over the conversation with your child as well— and not just to describe the problem areas; make a point to share the positive information you've heard. In a case where a teacher hasn't provided you anything positive, ask how your child is doing. You want to make sure that you do as much reinforcing of proactive behavior as you do managing and correcting performance problems.
- Homework each night requires a structured process you incorporate and manage. Create a homework schedule with

your child that works. This means a set time when homework is going to start every day. It can't happen right after school because everyone needs some time to relax from school. This means your child needs to go out and play, talk to friends, get away from the school process. Take that into consideration and then identify a specific time every day to do homework and stick to it. However, this process has to begin before 7:00 p.m. and with younger children, start earlier.

- When you start hearing, "We didn't have homework tonight" or "We did it at school," ask to see what they did in school. Any homework done in school needs to be reviewed by you at home. You've got to be in control and manage the process. Remember that a week of incomplete assignments means your child is going to have to double his efforts the following week. Keep in mind your child dislikes doing homework. Doing twice as much as he needs to because you haven't managed the process creates a bigger problem for him and you. Be consistent; there's homework each night, expect it to be completed.

- Every child has a subject she doesn't do well in and, as a result, it's going to be the one that gets the least attention, which causes her to fail. Therefore, work on the most difficult subjects first. Remember that keeping the more difficult subjects until later in the process oftentimes creates problems between you and your child as fatigue and frustration set in, which is where arguments arise. Although your child's never going to be happy to do homework, she is clearly going to have more energy at the beginning of the process than at the end. Save homework assignments in her stronger subjects until later on in the process—they're easier for her and get done quicker.

- Young children need close supervision, so the best place to do homework is at the kitchen table, where they can get any help they need quickly. Older children, based on the responsibility they demonstrate, can often do their homework in their room. However, remember that for many children that room has a number of distractions. Today it's not unusual to find a child with their own computer, TV, cell phone, iPads, etc. So you have to manage the process. Homework time is time in which they're not going to be on their cell phones texting or sending emails to their friends, but completing work that's assigned. The quicker they complete homework, the more free time they have. However, it is the case that some kids *do* perform better with distractions, with music or TV on. The key is to see what works best and then to manage the process to get the best results from your child.

- As the homework manager, your job is to review the work and suggest changes. Again, here's where leadership and follow-through are important. Make sure that completed work goes in the completed homework folder and gets back to class. Also, if you find that your child is particularly disorganized, you may want to check that folder before it leaves the home and make sure everything you put in last night is ready to go to school. Also, remind the child he needs to turn in the homework each day. Oftentimes a child has completed his homework, and the problem is he just didn't turn it in. So, again, you've got to drive the process and follow up.

- Make a point to show your child her results. Get her to recognize that her grades improved because of her attention to homework.

Okay, by this time you may be asking, "Well if I do all of this, how does my child become responsible for his or her work? It should be his or her responsibility to complete his or her homework." Answer: The reason you're doing this is because your child has already proven to you he or she is not responsible; that's why you're involved. You're closely monitoring the process so that the homework is completed and turned in, all of which will positively impact your child's grade. Where's responsibility? You're teaching it. Remember, learning to be responsible isn't a product; it's not like buying a stereo or loaf of bread. It's a process and takes place over time, but it needs close attention, management, and supervision to achieve the results you expect.

CHAPTER 7

Bully-Proofing Your Child

"Teaching prejudice to a child is itself a form of bullying. You've got to be taught to hate."
—ROGER EBERT

Jim sits on a bench each day alone at recess and reads while his classmates play. He's always the last one picked when kids divide up to play games because the kids know he's not athletic and is afraid of being hurt. As a result, he's an easy target.

Bob, Jan, and De have something in common with Jim. Their classmates all constantly torment them for being different.

Bob was the largest kid in first grade, an easy twenty pounds heavier than his fellow classmates, and each year he put on more weight. As a result, Bob moved slowly and was a constant subject of ridicule, not included and always picked on.

Jan reached puberty early; when all students returned to fourth grade, everyone noticed Jan was notably different than all her female classmates, and as she continued to develop throughout the next several years, consistently hiding herself in oversized clothing, she was taunted and made fun of by girls and boys alike.

From second grade until she graduated, De was the tallest kid in school. She towered over her classmates, and unfortunately her coordination didn't develop along with her size, which often caused her to trip and have difficulty walking and running. Added to this was De's wardrobe; she often wore her older siblings' much smaller hand-me-downs, which further emphasized De's height, making her a constant target.

What do these children have in common? Yes, they've been bullied, they're victims, but what makes them victims? A sign on their back or a badge that says, "I'm less than you, kick me, laugh at me, make fun of me?"

Experts tell us that kids who are bullied are often isolated, insecure, small, weak, and can't defend themselves. They have difficulties making friends, give up easily, and are under-socialized. They can't stick up for themselves, don't deal with disappointments well. Or they may be a physical target because of their manner of dress, the way they communicate, their size, or they may demonstrate a learning or behavioral challenge.

In short: a child who sticks out, who looks different, acts different, is awkward, who is under-socialized, or one who comes from a different environment, state, community, country, speaks a different language, or has a different skin color. So they're the target!

All of these things make them different, but different enough to pick on? One thing's for sure, they didn't ask to be different, they didn't ask to stick out. They don't know how to fix this but want to, and they certainly didn't ask for the abuse they received. Sometimes this results in disastrous decisions and outcomes.

Emilie Olsen, a thirteen-year-old middle school student, was constantly bullied by classmates in school and online due to her race and perceived sexual orientation. Emilie wrote to a friend on Facebook, "I'm causing all of this trouble," and "It hurts when you have to explain yourself to people you don't know or don't like. You feel them judging you, staring at you, talking about you, and I've made up my mind, I want to die." On December 11, 2014, Emilie killed herself with her father's gun.

So who puts the target on their backs? Who's responsible for the Emilies, Jims, Bobs, Jans, and Des and the thousands of other children and adolescents who feel bullied and harassed from the time they enter school until the time they complete it? What effects does this have on them, their self-esteem, their willingness to risk, embrace new opportunities, or experience success in school, relationships, and careers?

Fixing the bullying epidemic in this country may not be an easy problem to solve, but it's one that needs to be addressed. It can be stopped by incorporating a different view of the victims, bullies, and others who may be responsible.

To begin with, let's look at bullying from a different perspective. Being a bully or a victim isn't a birthright. It's a learned behavior and one, unfortunately, taught by parents. Not necessarily by intent so much as by omission. Once again, parents aren't paying attention. They forgot about a responsibility they have to their children: to help them be protected and accepted. Parents need to recognize that "bully-proofing" their children begins at home.

First, parents need to realize they're the ones responsible for putting the "kick me" poster on the backs of their children or suggesting in some cases that it is okay to be the one who does the kicking.

Over the past twenty-five years, thousands of parents have addressed this issue with our counselors at Outreach Concern. "You need to help my son who's being bullied in the classroom, my daughter's being picked on by the 'mean girls' on the playground." In every case, the parents have been correct. Their children are being bullied and picked on and singled out. The problem is that parents are responding too late, failing to realize that they've been part of the equation.

No, not by choice—they didn't decide they wanted their children to be picked on. But not paying attention to the clues and nuances their children demonstrated long before they entered school has led to them becoming a target. In short, if parents would have paid closer attention to the behaviors their children demonstrated before they entered a new world, their children wouldn't be victimized or demonstrate the inappropriate behavior that bullies portray.

No, not all children need to look, sound, and be the same; they are entitled, however, to demonstrate a presence that helps them successfully negotiate the new environment they have to contend with, armed with skills that allow them to compete successfully with their peers.

So what should parents do? The first step is to go back to the guidelines of *21st Century Parenting*, but in this case, parents need to look at their children's personal environment and behaviors: what and how they present themselves to their audiences. Remember that most of this is in evidence before a child enters the classroom.

The first people to see what children present are moms and dads. The parent who waits for their child to enter the new environment of school under the assumption that it is there that he or she will develop the skills to help them navigate it successfully have already established a losing situation for their child. Sure, schools have anti-bullying programs. But, by not recognizing what their child enters school *with*, parents have already put the "victim-bully" label on their child before he or she becomes part of that new world. When parents don't start bully-proofing early, not paying attention to the actions and behavior their children demonstrate, they develop a negative life script that's easy for others to see and respond to and difficult for them to alter.

Remember the readiness training addressed in an earlier chapter. It was aimed at helping your children develop a bridge between home and school, to help them feel comfortable and safe on entering a new environment. Bully-proofing is part of readiness training, providing your child with the additional skills that keep them from being viewed as passive, shy, and helpless, lacking in confidence, and thus becoming the perfect target. Bully-proofing your children helps them develop the confident, considerate, and assertive presence they need to have to navigate throughout their new society, as well as preparing them for what lays ahead in their future.

Once again, those first five or six years before a child enters school are when parents need to teach children how to be effective, assertive, social creatures: how to treat others, what to expect in return, how to deal with conflict and confrontation, how to share, and how to compete.

Bully-proofing your children teaches them to compete on an equal playing field with their peers in and out of school and helps to make sure they don't project a presence that supports them in being taken advantage of or encourages them to take advantage of others. In short, recognize that it's your responsibility to teach your children to be an assertive, considerate, and self-confident individual before they enter school. Don't set your child up to be bullied or to be a bully due to your lack of involvement.

Recognize these are learned behaviors. A child learns to be helpless, frightened, risk avoidant, and passive from a parent who either demonstrates similar behaviors or doesn't see it as their responsibility to teach their children how to incorporate an assertive presence. Each of these skills is essential in socializing children to walk into school and feel they have a right to be there. To put up their hand when they think they have an answer to a question and not feel demoralized if they're incorrect.

The child who learns how to win, how to lose, how to play, and how to be considerate and grateful is set up to be successful for the rest of his life. He looks forward to school, to competing with himself and others; he develops friendships and doesn't personalize disappointment. The child who stands on his own two feet can only begin when parents recognize it's his responsibility to direct those feet in the right direction.

A child who learns to be helpless at home as a result of parents not teaching her how to risk and be successful, how to deal with disappointment as well as successes, is put behind the socializing "eight ball." Waiting until your child enters school, assuming she'll learn these skills in the classroom, will come up short every time.

When should this begin? Early. Because a child learns to be a victim or bully early and has time to practice from the time he or she is born throughout the rest of his or her life.

So before you call your child's school and complain that your son or daughter is being bullied, ask yourself: how long have you known this? When did your child become a target, and what have you done to keep that from happening? Have you armed your son or daughter with the ability to feel accomplished, successful, to compete, and risk? It's never too late to start, of course, and your children will thank you for this for the rest of their life.

So, let's get started again.

Bully-proofing your child begins with the Bully-Proofing Check Sheet. Our experience in working with thousands of kids in the educational community tells us that kids who get bullied are targets because of the way they look, act, and respond. By incorporating the points in this check sheet as part of your child's readiness training, you take the target opportunity away from potential bullying.

Children who learn these skills and practice them—under parental direction—doesn't need their school to bully proof them because they enter school with an assertive, straightforward posture that makes them take responsibility for their behavior. They speak up when they believe they've been wronged and rely on themselves rather than others to make them feel whole, confident, capable, and accomplished. Below are twelve simple steps you can incorporate into your family's life every day to bully-proof your child.

Bully-Proofing Check Sheet

1. Teach your child proper hygiene. A child who comes to school clean, with teeth brushed, hair combed, and clean clothes that fit is less likely to become a target.
2. Teach your child to speak clearly and directly when spoken to by adults or other children.
3. Teach your child proper eye contact and to look up, not down.
4. Teach your child to be assertive and speak up.
5. Teach your child proper posture, to stand up straight with his shoulders back.
6. Teach your child how to stand up for himself.
7. Teach your child to be appreciative of others and to express that appreciation.
8. Teach your child to accept the differences of others.
9. Teach your child to be aware of how his behavior affects others.
10. Teach your child how to problem-solve.
11. Teach your child fair play and how to compete with good sportsmanship.
12. Teach your child kindness, care, consideration, and courtesy for others.

Yes, this might seem overwhelming. *How do I teach my child all of these behaviors?* you may ask. Remember that you have five years to model, teach, and practice before your child enters school. You then have the next thirteen years to reinforce the behaviors you want your child to demonstrate the rest of his life. A child who learns these skills early and practices through parental direction won't need his school to teach him, because he'll enter school with an assertive posture already, taking responsibility for his behavior, speaking up when he believes he's been wronged, and reliant on himself rather than others to make him feel whole, confident, capable, and accomplished—and this lasts for the rest of his life.

CHAPTER 8

Who's in Charge of Your Family's Technology?

"It's very important that children learn to use technology—it's part of life—but also that they learn when to put it down."
—ANNE WOJCICKI

Matt is a seventeen-year-old high school student with too much time on his hands. He pulls up his school online with a map of the campus, wondering, if he were going to blow up the school, where would he hide the bombs? He indicates on the map where he'd place the explosives. A week later, a man in Philadelphia is investigating high schools for his son. On his computer he pulls up the school site Matt attends, sees the map with bombs indicated at various locations on the campus, and immediately contacts the FBI. Matt is arrested, his computer equipment confiscated. He and his parents go through an expensive litigation process resulting in Matt being placed on probation for five years, and he is expelled from school.

Today children and adolescents spend on the average of five-and-a-half hours each day online—texting, FaceTiming, Snapchatting,

Instagramming, and gaming. They are far less involved with exercise, play, family, and friends. Whether this is good or bad depends in large part on how they utilize the technology they have access to; the benefits versus the dangers they're exposed to, or how much such use supports or detours them in developing other necessary skills for their success. In Matt's case, his involvement costs time, considerable financial impact to his family, and his freedom.

Technological advances grow and develop at an increasingly fast pace. What's innovative today is outdated next week. However, there are two aspects that are constant that every parent needs to be aware of when it comes to their child's use of technology.

The first is easy. Once introduced to the high-tech world, children learn how to negotiate through it quickly, as if it was part of their DNA. In many families, children are so tech-savvy they become the family IT experts for all the new technology brought into the home.

The second aspect, however, is a bit more difficult. It's the impact children's technological behavior can have on themselves and others. This, unfortunately, is the part that they don't develop easily, and one that often leads to difficulties. It's where they make decisions regarding their technology use that often has a serious impact and consequences in their lives. Here's where parents need to pay attention to their child's technology behavior because children don't get it, they don't think it through, and they don't recognize how their decisions and actions regarding their technology use can have an impact on themselves and others, sometimes for the rest of their lives.

In March 2011, an East Los Angeles college student posted a video online complaining about the "hordes of Asians" enrolled at UCLA and said they had interrupted her library studies with cell phone calls about a tragedy in Japan. Her video received worldwide attention, resulting in her receiving death threats and later causing her to withdraw from school.

In January 2010, fifteen-year-old Phoebe Prince took her life as a result of being bullied online and in person by fellow classmates. The nine teenagers involved later faced legal charges, including assault, stalking, and violation of civil rights resulting in injury, criminal harassment, and delinquency.

Eighteen-year-old Ally Pfeiffer found a Facebook profile substituting her picture with a photograph of a cow, making fun of her weight. A police investigation identified two former classmates of Ally's who were charged with criminal impersonation and second-degree harassment.

These examples point toward the devastating effects people's technological behavior can have on their lives and those of others. The consequences for all involved can and did have a serious impact on their future lives.

So who's in charge of technology at your house, and how is it being utilized? Allowing technology to be the caretaker of your child hours upon hours each day incorporates outside influences into your child's life that becomes his or her mainstay of information, guidance, and direction. Unfortunately, many times the actions children demonstrate, like those in the previous examples, are based on what they're exposed to, and they can have a serious, negative effect on their present and future life. Therefore, parents need to control technology and recognize it as a privilege they offer to their children, not a right. And that the parent holds the right of refusal of that privilege, which needs to be exercised based on the behavior their child demonstrates.

Casey is twelve years old and in the eighth grade. He is the eldest of three children, a good student, social, plays sports, and gets along well with his family. Around 4:00 in the afternoon, his mother is looking for her children and enters Casey's room where her son and daughter are watching TV. Opening the door, she finds Casey quickly adjusting his pants.

Mom inquires what the kids were doing and Casey sheepishly responds, "Nothing," as his sister jumps into Mom's arms. Mom separates the children and begins to question both of them. Casey sticks to his story. His sister eventually says Casey and she were playing a game where they took down each other's pants. Later, Mom tells her husband what had happened and they both question Casey, who finally admits they were touching each other, but had their underwear on. More questioning and various stories result in the parents taking their children to a psychologist, who uncovers Casey has been molesting his sister for the past six months. Child Protective Services is contacted, both children get involved in counseling, and some legal action is taken against Casey. During counseling it is discovered that Casey had been introduced to a pornographic website by a friend several months earlier and has it on his cell phone. Initially, he admits only to looking at it once or twice, but later it's discovered he has ninety-five pornographic apps on his phone and twenty-five sites on his laptop that he has been visiting daily.

The long-term impact of this situation on the family—and Casey's sister, in particular—remains to be seen. However, the action the parents took was a major step in the right direction. Casey's parents were involved, caring, supportive, and active in their children's lives. They work hard to maintain a good home life for themselves and their children. They chose to make a tough—but *correct*—decision, one that would be difficult for any parent to make. In doing so they confronted a problem that was costly, emotional, and impacted the whole family, but necessary in taking a strong position toward recovery.

Casey's parents thought they paid attention to their children. But in this case, they weren't paying *enough* attention. All parents need to be hypervigilant about what's going on in their child's technological world, and to know who and what's influencing them, consistently paying attention to their child's environment and what they're exposed to.

What exactly should parents pay attention to regarding technology? Any and all technology their children have access to. Parents need to recognize that all technology influences their children in some way, so here are some questions to pay attention to: How much time do they spend online, texting? Who are they talking to and what are they talking about? Who is influencing them, and how is that influence being manifested in their behavior? How much time do they spend in their room isolated online to the exclusion of family, outside relationships, or extracurricular activities? How is their technology exposure influencing their behavior, and is it counterproductive to developing other skill sets necessary for their success? The wrong technology decision a child makes can have a far-reaching consequence on the rest of his or her life.

The answer to who's in charge of technology is the person who pays for it, who understands it, and who can make technology decisions in the best interest of his or her child and family when his or her child can't. The answer should be clear, be in charge of your children's technological life before their technology choices impacts their life and others.

Recognize that technology in the hands of a child or adolescent can be an asset or a liability. Unfortunately, children don't recognize how far-reaching the wrong technological choices can be. The following five steps can help parents pay attention and remain in charge of their children's technology world, supporting and protecting them in making choices in their best interest.

Five Steps to Taking Charge of Technology:

1. Consistently monitor your child's technology use.
2. Identify apps to install on cell phones, computers, laptops, and tablets. That will help you control and monitor what comes in and goes out of your child's technological world.

3. Create a healthy balance between your child's technology use and real-life activities like playing with friends, being outside, enjoying sports, and other extracurricular activities.

4. Discuss technology use AND misuse with your children. Set up and enforce clear consequences for irresponsible technology use.

5. Remember, your child's technology use is a privilege, not a right. You hold both the right and the privilege.

CHAPTER 9

Helping Your Child Off the Merry-Go-Round

"There are challenges, especially within the framework of divorce, when parental guilt can sometimes blur what should be the best decision."
—LZ GRANDERSON

Laura and Bob have been divorced for twenty years. They have two children, Annie and Ed. Unfortunately, consistent conflict, a bitter custody battle, and ongoing fighting after the divorce led to two decades of battling between the parents and extremely negative experiences for their children, who have since both married and divorced. Ed, the older of the two children, is now on his second marriage.

Each year, over one million American children experience the divorce of their parents. These children are seven times more likely to suffer from depression, are more at risk to have suicidal thoughts, and have an increased risk of chemical dependency. Studies suggest that teenagers from divorced families are more likely to experience academic and behavioral issues, higher dropout rates in school, and self-esteem and interpersonal relationship problems. These are all reasons for divorcing parents to pay attention to their child's CDC Family domain.

It seems ironic how the institution that often leads to the creation of children and families also serves to impact their very success. Although the number of couples marrying is declining, the number divorcing isn't, with even second marriages failing at a 60 percent rate.

Today, 40 percent of children are products of divorce, which has created a variety of family systems: divorcing, divorced, single parent, and blended families all sharing children. In some cases, parents share custody of their children equally, carting them back and forth like some nomadic tribe. Other custodial arrangements vary in time and involvement, all creating scenarios that move children from various situations, oftentimes making it difficult for them to juggle their lives, let alone the difficulties they experience due to whatever conflict their parents have introduced.

Then there's remarriage, creating various families of his, hers, mine, and ours. This is exacerbated further by the fact that 60 percent of second marriages fail, which often leads to other family arrangements, such as a third or fourth marriage, which have an even higher failure rate. All the while, dragging children through what can be an emotional minefield, adding additional issues and difficulties to their Core Development Components.

Involved parents who recognize how difficult this can be for their children often work hard to create a healthy emotional transition. All too often, however, divorcing parents exhibiting irrational behavior toward each other don't pay attention to the fact their children often lack the coping skills to deal with the emotional turmoil they experience. As a result, children and adolescents are experiencing something they didn't sign up for—the breakdown of what was supposed to be the most secure environment in their lives.

In short, they've been thrown a curve. The parents they were supposed to count on for support and security are now in crisis, impacting the very system established to get their needs met. Often their experience results in various emotional or behavioral changes that impact their ability to demonstrate appropriate performance in school and at home, as well as carry on with the normal everyday operation of their lives.

Too many parents don't realize the extent of emotional upheaval their children are exposed to—first when their parents start to drift apart in a preseparation situation, then the divorce itself, with their parents sometimes displaying aggressive, hostile, uncaring, and nonsupportive behavior to one another. Unfortunately, these behaviors often continue through a difficult custody battle and single parenthood, all impacting a child's emotional temperature and personal competency.

Complicating this further, some parents carry on a lifelong battle with their ex-spouse that can sometimes resembles a hockey match, with their children being the puck slammed from one parent to another. Adding to the emotional turmoil, sometimes parents expose their children too early to new relationships and possibly even remarriage, establishing an emotional roller-coaster for all involved. For some children, childhood is nothing more than coping with their parents' "Merry-Go-Round," further impacting their lives, giving them a somewhat skewed picture of what marriage, family, and relationships are all about; often this impacts them in their own adult relationships, causing them to project a lack of commitment due to viewing such relationships as disposable.

This is not a condemnation of divorce and remarriage or a suggestion that parents need to stay together when they are in an unhealthy or unattainable relationship. However, it is important to note the experiences that children endure as a result of these situations cause a heightened degree of emotionality that often manifests itself with problems in the classroom, their home life, and personal relationships as emotional temperatures rise in reaction to families being pulled apart.

When parents go in and out of marriage, creating an emotional family roller-coaster, many kids learn that relationships are easily disposable, causing them to invest less in relationships as they get older. Most certainly a great number of them have issues regarding commitment and trust, further impacting their lives.

Children of divorced parents have mixed emotions about loyalty, honesty, credibility, and resentment. They fear for their own security and often feel unimportant in the family scheme of things, which threatens their own emotional stability in ways they may carry throughout their life.

What can parents do? First, recognize that although no one should stay in a bad relationship, as long as there are children in the family, they are going to be impacted. Therefore, demonstrating an awareness and consideration for their position, helping them transition through this process should be of major concern.

Schools need to know what's going on and teachers need to be informed, so they can read what's going on behaviorally in these children in order to make appropriate accommodations. Sometimes counseling is a good idea. In short, providing for the ongoing needs of your child who will be in crisis along with you, yet without the developed coping skills to deal with his or her emotions.

If you don't want your children to become collateral damage as a result of your divorce, don't involve them in the fighting, lying, battling, and blaming that goes on between you and your spouse. Don't use them as pawns in your conflict. Try to keep their lives as normal as possible as you resolve your relationship problems.

In a perfect world, you keep as much of your relationship issues between you and your soon-to-be-ex-spouse as is possible. Realistically, in many cases, this is difficult; however, consider the impact your behavior has on your child. The immediate and long-term effect can leave a lasting and sometimes costly impact on his or her life.

Developing an awareness of your children's world in relationship to the dysfunctional family system they're now involuntarily a part of will help you make better choices and accommodate their needs, getting them off the emotional roller-coaster they didn't ask to be part of and don't deserve to be affected by.

CHAPTER 10

Failure to Launch

*"I can accept failure, everyone fails at
something. But I can't accept not trying."*
—Michael Jordan

*Shawn is twenty-five and has barely completed two semesters
of college. He's never been able to hold a job longer than a few
months, lives in his parents' garage, and spends his afternoons
getting high with his friends. Jan graduated from high school
with honors, got a scholarship to a prestigious university,
joined a sorority, and found out about what having too much
fun in college results in—she lost her scholarship and ended
up back home with her parents. Gene graduated from college
and was hired by a large retail firm, but was let go six months
later as a result of her constant absences and inconsistent work
performance.*

What do all these kids have in common? They all came from good
homes, with parents who cared and were involved, but they all seem to
have difficulty successfully getting off the launching pad into adulthood
hyperspace. The Shawns, Jans, and Genes make up an ever-growing
population of about eighteen million young adults who return to the nest

soon after leaving high school or college or who have run into difficulty with their newfound independence.

We're not talking about the thousands of college graduates who return home as a result of not being able to secure a job or experience economic difficulties due to student loan debt or are just not able to make ends meet.

These other young adults didn't make it due to their lack of direction, consistency, commitment, and self-discipline, all resulting in returning to "planet parent." In many cases it's a matter of just not knowing how to make it on their own. Or a continued over-dependency on parents, and the belief the entitled lifestyle they experienced for eighteen years should just continue, refusing to discipline themselves to a new set of adult norms connected to a society far less forgiving than their parents. As a result, they are a part of that fraternity of learned helpless young adults who've now chosen to elongate their adolescence by looking for their parents to support this fantasy, and unfortunately, many parents do.

The important thing for parents to realize is this doesn't have to happen, and when it does, there's an answer. Let's face it, not all kids are the same; some mature quicker than others, and some for various reasons aren't ready for the independence of adulthood. So returning to planet parent doesn't mean the launch was a total failure—that is, unless the passengers are intending to take up permanent residency.

Parents need to realize that parenting doesn't end when your child reaches eighteen; it just needs to take on a new form. The question is what form or direction has to do with the behavior and relationship your adult child demonstrates. As many parents will attest, the magical age of eighteen may bring adult status in legal terms, but it doesn't necessarily correlate with good decision-making, responsibility, or success.

Parents who embrace the *21st Century Parenting* model, however, witness their children demonstrate a strong sense of discipline in various aspects of their life, supporting their present and future success. Even if they return home to get some help, they recognize it's for temporary support from parents with their goal to get back on the launching pad with a new plan toward their independence.

Like Jill, who was a strong high school student, graduated from college, and moved up to Northern California. After graduation she got a great job with a marketing firm. Enjoying her newfound independence, Jill seemed to be on a trajectory toward success. Unfortunately, a year into her job she got laid off. That put Jill back in the job market at a time when unemployment was high and, for an inexperienced newcomer, prospects were scarce. At about the same time, Jill broke up with her boyfriend, but not before the two had acquired a considerable amount of debt.

Jill was embarrassed, but called her parents asking for their help. They all agreed moving home was the best answer. However, both Jill and her mother were concerned about her reentering the home, due to the somewhat shaky relationship the two had during Jill's last few years of high school. Jill's goal, from the time she moved back home, was to be back out on her own. Before she moved in she sat down with her parents and identified a two-year plan, which incorporated paying off her debts and finding a job.

Her parents recognized reinvesting in their daughter was good for everyone. They loaned her money so that she could get away from high interest payments and worked out some money management issues to help her with her financial future.

Jill wanted to enroll in a graduate program she believed would further her marketability. Her parents agreed and helped her with tuition. Jill got a part-time job working about twenty-five hours a week and became a certified yoga instructor teaching classes on the weekends. During that year,

Jill repaired her relationship with her mother. She managed to pay back a good deal of the loan from her parents, completed half of her graduate program, and by the year's end had gotten back on her feet. Jill found a new job, but instead of moving out, negotiated a six-month stay with her parents so she could build up her financial war chest. She finished her graduate program, got promoted, paid her parents off, and moved into a little apartment.

As a parent of a returning young adult, you've got to figure out what your role is: advisor, consultant, director—in many cases, banker—or all of the above. The question is what kind of relationship can you establish with your adult child? Is it a cooperative relationship where everyone sits down and creates a workable plan that's focused on getting your child back on his or her own? Or do you have to take a more aggressive approach, because unlike Jill, your adult child is unwilling to work with you and commit to a plan that may mean changing his or her behavior and incorporating new steps toward his or her emancipation and independence?

Mom and Dad, remember: you're still the parent, you still get to make the ultimate decisions in your home as to whether the welcome sign is out or you change the locks on the doors. One of the questions you have to pose is how far are you willing to go to protect and support your adult child from the mistakes they've made and make sure the actions and behaviors they bring home won't impact the current status of household.

Bob, twenty-two, was a good athlete in high school and a talented artist who convinced his parents to enroll him in a prestigious out-of-state art school. Over the next three years, Bob jumped from art school to architecture school to engineering to design school, with his parents constantly writing checks for his bad choices and growing expenses and seeing little return on their investment. During this time there were constant conversations with Bob regarding his lack of progress; his parents saw little change but heard many excuses for his lack of responsibility and unwillingness to finish what he started.

Frustrated, Bob's parents looked for some help. The advice they got was initially difficult for them to accept, but after realizing what they were doing was nothing but cosigning Bob's behavior, they realized a stronger approach was a necessary course of action.

Their initial plan was to sit down with Bob and discuss helping him reorganize his life, get focused, and complete school. They wanted Bob's input to see what his plans were and how he viewed his current situation. Initially Bob was unwilling to sit down with his parents. Finally they got together to discuss options like possibly moving back home, looking into community college, getting a part-time job—taking some steps to identify and work toward goals that would be beneficial to both Bob and his parents. Halfway into the conversation Bob blew up and walked out complaining his parents had no interest in his future and were uncaring and unfair.

His parents made a few additional attempts to get him back to the negotiating table, all of which failed. Finally, the ultimatum was for him to come home and discuss alternatives or they would cut him off. Bob refused and later found the rest of his belongings in four large black plastic bags outside his parents' home with a note that said, "When you're ready to talk to us we're ready to listen." Angry, Bob wasn't heard from for about two months. Then his parents finally got a phone call from him, and the three sat down and developed a plan geared toward his success.

If that sounds like too much tough love, remember what's going on. In this case, Bob's self-esteem, perception, and motivation are all impacted because of his lack of accomplishments, and Bob doesn't recognize it. Bob's lack of commitment to focus on issues he was experiencing with CDCs were causing him to jump from one opportunity to the next, with no sense of commitment or discipline. As long as his parents continue to support his actions and cosign his indecisive behaviors, he continued to come up short from a performance standpoint.

You can't always guarantee your children are going to have a successful launch into adulthood; it's possible they may get a little off course. Here's where you may need to get back onboard and take over controls, as Bob's parents did. But remember that the eventual goal is to turn over those controls to your adult child who, as he or she starts demonstrating success, will be happy to enjoy that success.

How do you insure yourself and your adult child against failure to launch? Remember it's never too late to apply the principles of *21st Century Parenting*. The same principles that you would incorporate from childhood through adolescence work with adults. Help your adult child achieve success by using the first R, Reading Your Environment to identify which of the CDCs are in conflict and how many impact other areas of your adult child's world. Now let's incorporate the second R, Regulating Emotional Temperature. As a result of the dysfunction your adult children are demonstrating, how is their behavior affecting themselves or others? How are they dealing with the conflict and disappointment they're experiencing as a result of their dysfunction? Keep in mind that it's very possible they don't recognize the CDC dysfunction, as Bob didn't at all, which further acerbates the situation. Now, let's incorporate the third R, to Redirect your young adult's behavior to success.

Remember it's their lack of accomplishments that impacts how they feel about themselves and further affects their ability to perform. Now it may be necessary just to read the steps they're taking to achieve performance, particularly if they can actually recognize what good performance looks like.

That's where parental leadership comes back into play, sometimes—in order to present things they don't see. In the case of both Jill and Bob, both clearly needed the support and parental direction to help them get back on track. In Jill's case, she recognized that through no fault of her own, her efforts weren't directing down the road to success she was attempting to achieve. In her case, she recognized she needed help and was willing to do what it took to reevaluate and work with her parents and adjusted her life to get on track.

In Bob's case, he chose to fight his parents' attempt to help him redirect his behavior, which resulted in them taking a more aggressive approach. However, in the end, he too realized he needed to take another look at his situation and incorporate a different approach, and with the support of his parents he got back on track.

Parents should realize that incorporating *21st Century Parenting* with their adult children who get off-track can be an excellent diagnostic tool in assessing what's going on in their world and identifying the necessary steps they need to take to change things—whether they agree or, in some cases, fight the obvious. The result is heightened self-esteem and concept, and motivation to continue to demonstrate the success they're capable of. Additionally, part of the goal parents need to attain is teaching their young adults how to use *21st Century Parenting* independent of them, getting them to take charge and incorporate these steps in every aspect of their own lives, ultimately supporting their continued success.

Back to Readiness Training

Does it seem a little late in the game to talk about readiness training with your soon-to-be adult? It shouldn't because readiness training is all about accommodation, getting ready for that next step. Who's best at identifying what's next when it comes to your children, no matter what their age? You are. So just as readiness training is important in those early years through middle school and into high school, failure to launch in young adults indicates that readiness training is important in their lives too.

A way to guarantee a successful launch is to initiate a "Life after High School" conversation. Waiting until your young adult is confronted with the results of the poor decisions he's made after graduation is too late, often leading to arguments and disagreements for all involved. Therefore, having some frank discussions about your adolescent's expectations, goals, or how he might view his life after high school is a great way to minimize tough discussions after the fact and stimulate rewarding conversations to keep your adult child on track.

There are a number or reasons adults return home. But the four main reasons seem to relate to finances, being unprepared, not being able to balance their life, and a lack of self-discipline. Readiness training and the three Rs can assist parents in supporting their young adults in addressing each of these areas that negatively impact a successful launch-from-home to independence. Optimally, readiness training for young adults begins in their adolescence. Start conversations with them in their mid-teens around fifteen or sixteen before they leave the nest, so they have an idea of what lies ahead and what all involved can expect from one another.

These talks need to be conversational. You want to stimulate and support mutual interaction between you and your adolescent. You also want to be clear and specific about what you're capable of providing, as well as your expectations for his or her future and your part in it.

This can't be a lecture since you want the partnership and conversation of your young audience sharing their ideas, options, and expectations. This is a conversation that also needs to be revisited from time to time because your child's ideas and attitudes, along with objectives for what lies ahead, is going to change. Open communication about what lies ahead between your adolescent and you helps establish clear expectations and goals, as well as an understanding that when things don't work out, you are still there to help.

Sometimes saying no to your adult child who has failed at school or on the job may be one of the hardest things you've ever done, but it may also be the exact antidote your adult child needs in order to get reestablished.

> *Julie graduated from high school, enrolled in a private university, but didn't demonstrate the level of discipline needed to stay in school. Together with failing all of her coursework in the first semester, she developed an addiction to amphetamines, ultimately resulting in her leaving school. Julie's parents tried counseling and rehab programs, but these returned poor results due to Julie's lack of commitment. Julie would leave home for periods of time, then return, but refused to look for work or go back to school and was argumentative and generally demonstrated no commitment to work with her parents or change her behavior. Frustrated, Julie's mother woke her up early one morning, told her to get dressed, drove her to the local mall, and said, "Don't call me until you have a job." Two hours later, Julie had acquired a part-time job at one of the local eateries. A month later she was taken on full-time and promoted to assistant manager. Things got better; Julie decided she was going to get serious about school. With her parents help, she enrolled in a cosmetology program, got her license, and began to develop her business. Now she is married with a few kids of her own.*

No, there was no magic behind what happened in Julie's life—just that she was lucky enough that her parents decided they were no longer willing to put up with her behavior. In Julie's case, her parents literally pushed the three Rs down her throat; in doing so, they probably saved her life.

It's ultimately up to you, Mom and Dad, as to how much responsibility you choose to take on when your child fails to launch and returns to planet parent for whatever reason. The goal is to get them back to where they need to be, but in many cases, they aren't sure of exactly where that is or how to get there. However, by incorporating and teaching them how to effectively use the three Rs as a part of their decision-making process, both parent and child will achieve the long-term success that all parties are ultimately seeking.

Launching Off Contract

Remember your goal is not to punish or belittle, but to stimulate a different thought process that results in actions that lead to accomplishments, which in turn will increase your adult child's esteem, concept, and motivation to develop. In order to make this happen there has to be more than a conversation. The parties involved, parents and young adult, need to commit to actions that result in your adult child's emancipation and success and your satisfaction with his or her achieving whatever goals he or she has established for him- or herself.

You're entering into a business-like relationship with your adult child. So, to keep all parties involved in a new chapter of the family business, parents and adult children need to discuss developing a contract regarding those points, all agreed to. This contract needs to have clear, specific objectives, goals, and timelines that result in expected outcomes on behalf of all parties to the contract involved. Therefore, consider the following points in the contract you develop.

- *Develop a plan.* The adult and parent need to work cooperatively on developing a plan that incorporates a timeline to move out, educational opportunities or interests, career development, etc.— this plan should remain open to be reviewed and stressed as an open-ended conversation.
- *Timeline to leave.* There needs to be a clear, established timeline that both parent and adult child establish, resulting in the adult child emancipating himself from his dependency on his parents.
- *Educational requirements.* While at home, the adult child has to maintain an effort in school, either on a full- or part-time basis. On a part-time basis, no less than three classes a semester should be acceptable.

- *Employment requirements.* Full- or part-time employment must be maintained while living at home. This can also be the combination of part-time school and a part-time job with a minimum of no less than twenty-five hours per week employment.
- *No drug use or alcohol use at home.* If your adult child is over twenty-one, parent and adult should discuss what's acceptable alcohol use at home.
- *Establish boundaries.* Parent and adult child need to identify what are the acceptable rules and guidelines for living at home. Both parties need to have an appreciation for the maturity and expected behavior of all individuals living in the household.
- *Household expectations.* General household duties and responsibilities need to be clear and specific as to what's expected by all family members.
- *Curfew.* Parents and adult children need to agree upon a reasonable age-appropriate curfew that should support the needs and expectations for success while attending school or being employed.
- *Finances.* Financial need and responsibilities on the part of both parents and adult children need to be clear and explicit, as part of the contract, as to who is responsible for what. Any loans, tuitions, or financial responsibilities the adult child enters into with the parent should be identified. Addendums to the contract should be clear and explicit in terms of monies loaned and payback schedules.
- *Family participation.* Parents should be clear on their expectations of the adult child regarding involvement in family-related interaction.

Parents should support revisiting the contract throughout their adult child's time at home. Contracts are negotiable, and the goal should be to meet all points identified in the contract. When issues or opportunities present themselves that necessitate altering the contract, the interaction of both parents and adult child have to be considered. It's also highly important for parents to acknowledge progress and provide ongoing feedback to their adult child as she meet the goals identified in the contract or other opportunities that result in her accomplishments, all of which continues to establish and support a more aggressive approach toward success in whatever endeavor the adult child is embracing.

Besides achieving the goals identified in the contract leading to the independence of your adult child, this process stimulates a stronger bond, establishing a mutually beneficial relationship between parents and their adult children for the rest of their lives.

CHAPTER 11

21st Century Parenting in Review

*"There are only two lasting bequests we
can hope to give our children. One of
these is roots, the other, wings."*
—Johann Wolfgang von Goethe

Remember school, tests, midterms, finals? If you were like many of us, you looked forward to the review prior to the test so that you could cram to improve your grade. Unfortunately, there is no way to cram for the parent test. It's ongoing and all around you, lasting for eighteen years and beyond. Your final grade is what your child demonstrates as an adult and lives with him or her the rest of his or her life. So let's go back and review:

As parents, you need to recognize today that your kids bring more home and to the classroom, playground, and their social community than books, pencils, and iPads. Their emotional backpacks are often affected by family dysfunction, economic impact, physical challenges, learning disabilities, academic challenges, mental health issues, and various influences both in and outside the family, positive and negative, that often affect their ability to perform, feel good about themselves, develop relationships, and feel accomplished.

Today's performance in and outside of school requires more than the concept of the three Rs of yesterday. Although reading, writing, and arithmetic are important, today's expectations and future goals for children necessitate the need for a new set of three Rs, requiring parents to take a more active role in their children's life from infancy through adolescence, supporting their emancipation toward lifelong success. Simply put, doing what may have seemed easier fifty years ago now mandates recognizing and responding to the increasingly broad influences your children are exposed to, both good and bad, and establishing their ability to have the necessary tools to be effective, productive, and successful in negotiating their way through them.

So today it's not just children who need to pay attention, but parents as well—paying attention to what's going on in their children's world and what they're exposed to, and incorporating a new set of three Rs to assist in: *Reading Your Child's Environment*—paying close attention to the Core Development Constructs children operate around and what influences their behavior, performance, and success; *Regulating Your Child's Emotional Temperature*—paying attention to your children's responses in relationship to influences that stimulate their emotional temperature, as well as teaching them how to regulate their emotions and reactions to challenges and influences they are exposed to; and *Redirecting Your Child's Behavior*—paying attention to your children's accomplishments and disappointments and directing them toward their highest degree of personal success and significance.

In this process, parents need to recognize often unresolved and ongoing health, family, academic, behavioral, social, and emotional issues and how these can impact a child's attitude, behavior, and performance, causing emotional temperatures to rise and often having an impact on their child's success. As a result, they must recognize and respond to their child's needs as they develop along with their Core Development Competencies, creating a balance in their life leading to their present and future success.

Remember, emotional regulation is not a birthright, but a learned behavior. It is a parent's responsibility to develop their children's ability to control and regulate their emotional temperature in relationship to those issues they're exposed to throughout their life. Also, recognize that the absence of emotional control further impacts their children's safety, security, and success. Therefore, developing emotional regulation helps children recognize a responsibility to their behavior and how it impacts others in their society today and in their future.

Finally, the goal of a parent is to Redirect their child toward their highest level of personal competency. Recognize that self-esteem, self-confidence, and motivation aren't birthrights either. They too are learned, and only through achieving successes within his or her core competencies will the child be motivated toward continued success, establishing pride, assurance, and drive as a result of constant performance versus the shame, doubt, and stagnation he or she will feel due to a lack of accomplishments. And this can only be accomplished through parental attention—directing, guiding, and supporting their child's efforts toward positive accomplishments.

Simply put, today parenting is more than being your child's best friend or buying the latest technology. It's about leadership and paying attention, reading your child's environment, teaching him emotional regulation and redirecting him toward the development of his highest degree of personal competency and significance. It's also partnering with experts to support your child's development, safety, and success—because if you don't, no one else will!

Acknowledgments

Twenty-six years ago, I began writing *21st Century Parenting*, but didn't know it at the time. We introduced Outreach Concern, Inc., a fledgling nonprofit school-based counseling program, in Southern California in the fall of 1993. With twelve schools, fourteen counselors, and limited funds, we created an agency that emerged as one of the largest programs of its kind, serving over 890 schools, half a million children, adolescents, and families, and trained over 9,000 counselors. That experience led to the development of a new, highly successful school counseling intervention model that has now been adapted for parents in *21st Century Parenting*. To that end, I'm tremendously grateful for the commitment, support, and efforts of my team and staff, the hundreds of teachers, principals, and clinicians who championed our efforts in the schools we worked with, and for the results we achieved.

My sincere thanks to the Board of Directors of Outreach Concern, whose support for its mission has been the driving force behind the organization. I'm grateful to the many foundations over the years that recognized an investment in mental health services in schools produces a real return on investment in terms of the health, welfare, and success of the children in our school system. And most importantly, my love and appreciation to Mary, who along with Guss and Reggie, provided me the time, space, and support to complete this journey.

Bibliography

American Psychiatric Association, *Diagnostic and Statistical Manual of Mental Disorders*. Fourth Edition Text Revision. Arlington, VA: American Psychiatric Association 2007.

Associated Press. "Teen found dead in school bathroom of apparent suicide." *New York Post*, January 10, 2018, https://nypost.com/2018/01/10/teen-found-dead-in-school-bathroom-in-apparent-suicide/.

Botelho, Greg." Jaylen Fryberg: From Homecoming Prince to School Killer." *CNN*, October 24, 2014, https://www.cnn.com/2014/10/24/us/washington-school-shooter/index.html.

Brown, Brooks and Rob Merritt. *No Easy Answers: The Truth Behind Death at Columbine*. New York: Lantern Books, 2012.

Brown–Chidsey, Rachel, and Kristina J. Andren, eds. *Assessment for Intervention: A Problem-Solving Approach*. New York: Guilford Press, 2005.

Burch, A.D., and Patricia Mazzei. February 14, 2018. "Death Toll Is at 17 and Could Rise in Florida School Shooting," *New York Times*. https://www.nytimes.com/2018/02/14/us/parkland-school-shooting.html.

Christenson, S.L., and S.M. Sheridan. *Schools and Families: Creating Essential Connections for Learning* New York: Guilford Press, 2001.

Chuck, E., Johnson, A., and C. Siemaszko. February 14, 2018. "17 Killed in mass shooting at high school in Parkland, Florida." NBC News. https://www.nbcnews.com/news/us-news/police-respond-shooting-parkland-florida-high-school-n848101.

Dunst, C., Trivette, C. and A. Deal. *Enabling and Empowering Families: Principles and Guidelines for Practice*. Cambridge MA: Brookline Books, 1988.

Gendreau, L. 2010. "Conn. Woman Fights Back After Cyber Bullying." *NBC New York*, December 8. https://www.nbcnewyork.com/news/local/Conn-Woman-Fights-Back-After-Cyber-Bullying-111548429.html.

Green, Frank. "The Killer: Who Was He?" *Richmond Times–Dispatch*, 18 April 2007. www.timesdispatch.com/.

Hersey, Paul. *The Situational Leader*. New York: Warner Books, 1984.

Johnson, K., and S. Dewan. "Tangled Portrait of a Student Emerges in Washington Shooting." *New York Times*, 25 October 2014. https://www.nytimes.com/2014/10/26/us/contrasting-portraits-emerge-of-jaylen-ray-fryberg-shooter-at-washington-school.html.

Langman, Peter. *Why Kids Kill: Inside the Minds of School Shooters*. New York: Palgrave/Macmillan, 2009.

Lieberman, Joseph. *The Shooting Game: The Making of School Shooters*. Santa Ana, CA: Seven Locks Press, 2008.

Lovett, I. "UCLA Student's Video Rant Against Asians Fuels Firestorm." *New York Times*, 15 March 2011. https://www.nytimes.com/2011/03/16/us/16ucla.html?mtrref=www.google.com.

McPhate, M. "Wisconsin Prom Shooting Leaves Teenage Suspect Dead and Town Shaken." *New York Times*, 25 April 2016. https://www.nytimes.com/2016/04/26/us/wisconsin-prom-shooting-leaves-teenage-suspect-dead-and-town-shaken.html.

Myers, A.L. "LA School Shooting Was Accidental, 12-Year-Old in Custody." *US News & World Report*, 1 February 2018. https://www.usnews.com/news/best-states/california/articles/2018-02-01/suspect-arrested-in-shooting-at-los-angeles-middle-school.

O'Neill, A. "Court Filing Reveals Taunted Teen's Anguish in Final Hours." *CNN*, 9 April 2010. http://www.cnn.com/2010/CRIME/04/09/massachusetts.bullying.suicide/index.html.

Power, T., DuPaul, G.J. Shapiro, E.S. and A.E. Kazak. *Promoting Children's Health: Integrating School, Family and Community*. New York: Gilford Press, 2003.

Schweber, N., and M. Schwirtz. "Girl Fatally Stabbed at School in Connecticut on Day of Prom." *New York Times*, 25 April 2014. https://www.nytimes.com/2014/04/26/nyregion/connecticut-teenager-is-fatally-stabbed-by-fellow-student-police-say.html.

Shields, N. "2 Boys Charged in Plot." *Los Angeles Times*, 16 March 2005. http://articles.latimes.com/2005/mar/16/local/me-plot16.

Stephens, H.M. "Bibliography of Sir William Curtis (1752–1829)." 1888. http://www.curtis-curtiss.org/document_view.asp?id=110.

Tucson News Now Staff. "Sherriff Confirms 14-year-old Dies of Self-Inflicted Gunshot Wound at Cochise County School." *Tucson News Now*, 9 January 2018. http://www.tucsonnewsnow.com/story/37226015/school-shooting-cochise-county-coronado-elementary-lockdown-suicide-sierra-vista.

Shapiro, E., and W. Lloyd. "Indiana middle schooler returns to class with 2 guns, shoots peer, teacher: 'I was thinking, it's not real'." *ABC News*, 26 May 2018. https://abcnews.go.com/US/active-shooter-reported-indiana-middle-school-police/story?id=55413808.

Sheridan, S.M., and T.R. Kratochwill. *Conjoint Behavioral Consultation: Promoting Family–School Connections and Interventions.* New York: Springer, 2010.

Smith, M. "Indiana School Shooting: Teacher and Student Wounded; Gunman Detained." *New York Times*, 25 May 2018. https://www.nytimes.com/2018/05/25/us/noblesville-indiana-shooting.html.

US Department of Education Office of Communications and Outreach (2005). "Helping Your Preschool Child: With activities for children from infancy through age 5." https://www2.ed.gov/parents/earlychild/ready/preschool/preschool.pdf.

Valencia, N., Karimi, F., and H. Yan. 2018. "Texas school shooting: Sherriff says he doesn't believe any victims killed in crossfire with gunman." *CNN*, May 21. https://www.cnn.com/2018/05/21/us/texas-santa-fe-school-shooting/index.html.

Villafranca, O. "Santa Fe High School shooting suspect's father says son was bullied. CBS News, 21 May 2018. https://www.cbsnews.com/news/santa-fe-high-school-shooting-suspect-dimitrios-pagourtzis-victims-latest-2018-05-21/.

Webley, K. "Teens Who Admitted to Bullying Pheobe Prince Sentenced." *Time*, 5 May 2011. http://newsfeed.tim.com/201105/05/teens-who-admitted-to-bullying-phoebe-prince-sentenced/.